The Penguin Prac...
The TOEF...

Section 2
Structure and Written Expression

Daniel de Souza

PENGUIN BOOKS

PENGUIN BOOKS
Published by the Penguin Group
Penguin Books Ltd, 27 Wrights Lane, London W8 5TZ, England
Penguin Books USA Inc., 375 Hudson Street, New York, New York 10014, USA
Penguin Books Australia Ltd, Ringwood, Victoria, Australia
Penguin Books Canada Ltd, 10 Alcorn Avenue, Toronto, Ontario, Canada M4V 3B2
Penguin Books (NZ) Ltd, 182–190 Wairau Road, Auckland 10, New Zealand

Penguin Books Ltd, Registered Offices: Harmondsworth, Middlesex, England

Published by Penguin Books 1996
10 9 8 7 6 5 4 3 2 1
Text copyright © Daniel de Souza 1996
All rights reserved

The moral right of the author has been asserted

Printed in England by Clays Ltd, St Ives plc
Set in Garamond, Helvetica and Times

TOEFL is a registered trademark of Educational Testing Service
This publication has neither been reviewed nor endorsed by ETS

Introduction

The aim of this series of practice test papers is to prepare students for the TOEFL test (Test of English as a Foreign Language) and for this reason much care has been taken to ensure that it accurately reflects the format and level of actual tests. To achieve this the author has based the practice tests on a number of resources – ranging from actual test papers to American high school text books (since the ETS (Educational Testing Service), which administers TOEFL, also administers most of the American high school graduation tests).

Rather than repeat the information given out by the ETS in its brochures and bulletins, the aim of this introduction is to provide a more generalized overview of the test.

The TOEFL test is given, on a world-wide basis, twelve times a year. Although the primary purpose of a TOEFL certificate is to qualify foreign candidates for American universities, increasingly it is being used by government agencies, and multi-national and national companies, to test the fluency of potential employees.

How to Register

Registration forms are provided with the 'Bulletin of Information' published annually by the ETS and available from either local American schools or free of charge from TOEFL: CN 6151, Princeton, NJ 08541-6151, USA. Many people have complained that filling in the entry form is worse than taking the actual test; certainly much care and attention is required.

How to Complete Answer Sheets

Sample answer sheets are provided with each practice test book and consist of either vertical or horizontal columns of lettered ovals that have to be entirely filled in using a medium-soft lead pencil.

How to Prepare for the Test

Detailed strategies precede each volume of this series but some general tips follow.

- Stick to the stipulated time limits when using the practice tests.
- Become fully familiar with filling in the answer sheets. The tests are marked by computer and failure to fill in the oval spaces properly will lower your score.
- Ensure that you arrive at the test center on time and equipped with all the items listed in the 'Bulletin of Information'.
- Even if you have no idea what the answer is, never leave a question unanswered. With a twenty-five percent chance of guessing the correct answer, vital points can be earned in this manner.
- Since there is no limit to the number of times you can take the test, sitting a trial test will help you to familiarize yourself with both content and test procedures.

Scores

TOEFL is statistically scored to overcome the changing difficulty factor. Details on how to estimate your level from the practice tests can be found at the end of each book in the series.

Strategies for Section 2: Structure and Written Expression

Section 2 consists of sentences that test knowledge of important structural and grammatical elements of standard written English. These sentences cover a variety of subjects and give no special advantage to those versed in a specific field of study. Similarly, although the topics often refer to American and Canadian history and culture, knowledge of such matters is not required to answer the structural or grammatical points being tested.

The sample tests in this book are based on a library of actual tests going back five years and try to mirror both the standard and substance of recent TOEFL tests. The questions have been compiled to raise the areas of English structure and expression that have been most touched upon in recent test papers. To achieve this the questions from the test papers have been categorized according to the following specifications:

- repetition or deficiency of subject and verb
- verb agreement – tense and form
- full grammatical subordination
- correct use of ambiguous words
- pronoun form – agreement and reference
- correct relationships between phrases and clauses
- correct word order
- parallel structure
- needless repetition of words or phrases with identical meanings
- frequently confused words.

By using this method, a blue-print for all the practice tests in this book was constructed, with the forty questions in each test representing the most up-to-date equation of grammatical structures possible.

Section 2
Structure and
Written Expression

2

Time: 25 minutes (including the reading of the directions)
Now set your clock for 25 minutes.

This section is designed to measure your ability to recognize language that is appropriate for standard written English. There are two types of questions in this section, with special directions for each type.

Structure

Directions: Questions 1-15 are incomplete sentences. Beneath each sentence you will see four words or phrases, marked (A), (B), (C), and (D). Choose the <u>one</u> word or phrase that best completes the sentence. Then, on your answer sheet, find the number of the question and fill in the space that corresponds to the letter of the answer you have chosen. Fill in the space so that the letter inside the oval cannot be seen.

Example I   **Sample Answer**

The secretary of state -------   Ⓐ Ⓑ Ⓒ ●
on national TV tomorrow.

(A) he will be appearing
(B) appear
(C) who appears
(D) will be appearing

The sentence should read, "The secretary of state will be appearing on national TV tomorrow." Therefore, you should choose (D).

Example II   **Sample Answer**

How ------- after the flight?   Ⓐ Ⓑ ● Ⓓ

(A) the astronauts feel
(B) did feel the astronauts
(C) did the astronauts feel
(D) did the astronauts' feeling

The sentence should read, "How did the astronauts feel after the flight?" Therefore, you should choose (C).

Now begin work on the questions.

GO ON TO THE NEXT PAGE

2 2 2 2 2 2 2 2

1. The elephant uses its trunk ------- feeding to pull down branches and brush aside undergrowth enabling it to get to the most inaccessible leaves.

   (A) when
   (B) is
   (C) that it is
   (D) was

2. The Endangered Species Act of 1973 set forth the basic rules that apply in the US today but ------- curbs on travel companies selling big game hunting tours.

   (A) no
   (B) include
   (C) included no
   (D) are including

3. Warmer temperatures led to changes in the ecology of Europe, ------- the animal population and methods of hunting.

   (A) affecting
   (B) and affected
   (C) which affects
   (D) effecting

4. ------- world chess champion Bobby Fisher was a misogynist is well known but that hardly detracts from his astonishing ability.

   (A) That
   (B) Because
   (C) While
   (D) Being

5. Perhaps we should think in terms of bringing down unemployment ------- inflation at all costs.

   (A) then reducing
   (B) and reduce
   (C) although reduce
   (D) rather than reducing

6. In the aftermath of the Civil War, the 13th, 14th, and 15th Amendments to the Constitution ------- the mission of the Bill of Rights by abolishing slavery and by taking the first steps toward providing suffrage for citizens regardless of race.

   (A) continued
   (B) continuing
   (C) and continues
   (D) is continuing

7. The Piedmont Plateau supports Carolina's rich tobacco trade and, backed by cigarette profits, ------- the show piece of Winston-Salem.

   (A) Wake Forest College becoming
   (B) while Wake Forest College becomes
   (C) because Wake Forest College became
   (D) Wake Forest College has become

8. There are two basic fields of study that must be mastered to successfully complete the computer engineering course: software programming and -------.

   (A) hardware designing.
   (B) another that is hardware designing.
   (C) one is hardware designing.
   (D) also hardware designing.

GO ON TO THE NEXT PAGE

② ② ② ② ② ② ② ②

9. Although a hero of the 1812 war, Andrew Jackson was a peace loving man and only rarely ------- a gun after he became president.

   (A) he carried
   (B) did he carry
   (C) when he carried
   (D) that he carried

10. On most of the farms, ------- crop rotation is now computer guided for optimum timing and land usage.

    (A) even such age old techniques as
    (B) when even such an age old technique as
    (C) even such an age old technique as
    (D) even such an age old technique is

11. Neither the threat of another earthquake striking the region nor the high insurance premiums ------- to have deterred the influx of investors.

    (A) seem
    (B) and seems
    (C) but would seem
    (D) seems

12. Heart transplants, once considered a final desperate alternative, ------- that 60 percent of recipients can now expect to live more than a year after the operation.

    (A) which are now so successful
    (B) are now so successful
    (C) they are now so successful
    (D) is now so successful

13. The superior design of petroleum-powered vehicles ------- reflects years of research and refinement.

    (A) over electrically powered ones
    (B) more than electrically powered ones
    (C) above electrically powered ones
    (D) instead of electrically powered ones

14. In their current quest to create a drugless, crimeless, egalitarian society, the Swedish government ------- the entire population under constant electronic scrutiny.

    (A) opens and keeps
    (B) openly kept
    (C) openly keeping
    (D) openly keeps

15. ------- CNN's image as a global rather than American news gatherer, it has become more powerful than the Voice of America.

    (A) Since
    (B) As a consequence
    (C) However
    (D) Because of

GO ON TO THE NEXT PAGE

② ② ② ② ② ② ② ②

Written Expression

Directions: In questions 16-40 each sentence has four underlined words or phrases. The four underlined parts of the sentence are marked (A), (B), (C), and (D). Identify the <u>one</u> underlined word or phrase that must be changed in order for the sentence to be correct. Then, on your answer sheet, find the number of the question and fill in the space that corresponds to the letter of the answer you have chosen.

Example I

Sample Answer

Ⓐ Ⓑ ● Ⓓ

Because of the storm all fifteen of the car failed
<u>   </u>   <u>   </u>   <u>   </u>
    A   B   C

to reach the check point.
<u>   </u>
  D

The sentence should read, "Because of the storm all fifteen of the cars failed to reach the check point." Therefore, you should choose (C).

Example II

Sample Answer

Ⓐ ● Ⓒ Ⓓ

The development of the attack helicopter begins at
<u>   </u>   <u>   </u>
          A   B

the end of last year and was completed within six
<u>   </u>   <u>   </u>
    C   D

months.

The sentence should read, "The development of the attack helicopter began at the end of last year and was completed within six months." Therefore, you should choose (B).

Now begin work on the questions.

GO ON TO THE NEXT PAGE

2 2 2 2 2 2 2 2

16. It was once thought that Homer had never lived and that the poems ascribed to him
    A   B   C
    were of composing authorship.
           D

17. Having seen the man crossing the road and having heard the sound of his footsteps
                A   B
    coming up the stairs, Holmes knew it was him at the door.
         C   D

18. It is important for this venture to be adequately capitalized and financed if a
    A   B   C
    satisfactory conclusion is to be achieved.
             D

19. The newspaper published an article on how much money was he spending and
                 A   B
    included an analysis of his chance of being elected.
        C   D

20. It was stated in the report that, beside two properties in Dallas, a farm in the country
        A   B
    and several undeveloped plots of land were owned by the congressman.
          C   D

21. Now that work groups can conduct interactive conferences, paying no heed to
            A   B
    location, neither the distance nor the weather are important.
         C   D

22. It is believed that the entire crew of the submarine that impacted with the ocean bed
        A   B
    are dead and messages to this effect will be forwarded to their families.
        C   D

23. Today's announcement is clearly very good news of Hanscom Air Force Base and
            A   B
    the army's Natick Research Lab and very disappointing news for the Knight Naval
          C   D
    Air Station.

GO ON TO THE NEXT PAGE

②②②②②②②②

24. Despite political pressure from many major governments, so far no single company
    —————————————————————
              A
    from today's Singapore-based East European Banking Conglomerate including
    —————————
         B
    its Asian affiliate organizations are registered with the institution.
    ———————————————   ———————————————
              C   D

25. The Lab has a payroll of $57 million a year, earns a total $27 million a year in
    ———   ————————————————————————
     A   B
    pre-tax profits and it plays a significant role in the local economy.
    —————————————   ————————————————————
              C   D

26. Because of a growth hormone imbalance, even as a child, John Welsley was
    ——————————   ————————
         A   B
    far taller than everyone at the university.
    —————   ————————
      C   D

27. The producer of the OJ Simpson trial documentary television series said he
                         ———
                          A
    had been surprised at the world-wide interest shown which to date has resulted in
    ————————————————   ————————————————————
              B   C
    the series being screened by 82 countries.
    ————————————————————
              D

28. Toyota announced today that sales of vehicles to customers made in Japan
                                          ————————————————————————
                                                      A
    had increased by 10 percent over the last financial year while sales of American
    ——————————   ————————————
         B   C
    made vehicles had slumped.
    ————————————
         D

29. The bigger fluctuation on the New York stock exchange took place during the
        ——————   ——————————
          A   B
    Depression but the actual amount of share values gained and lost was a fraction of
                                                ————————————————————————
                                                            C
    today's average dealings.
    ——————————————
           D

30. Methods of temperature control vary but focus on preventing the fermenting liquids
    ——————————   ————————
         A   B
    from rising and to keep them at their optimum state of instability.
            ————————   ————————————————
               C   D

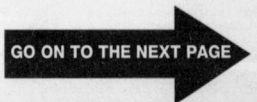

GO ON TO THE NEXT PAGE

10

2 2 2 2 2 2 2 2

31. Many doctors have only quite recently <u>began to appreciate</u> the potentials of the drug
A
<u>not only</u> in hastening a physiological cure but <u>improving</u> the psychological state of
B   C
<u>patients</u> as well.
D

32. <u>Other</u> overwhelmingly supported proposal was to link the foreign aid package to
 A
<u>a limiting of</u> the escalating arms purchases <u>even though</u> this <u>would</u> inevitably
B   C   D
damage the profits of US arms manufacturers.

33. <u>Australian wheat</u>, labelled a miracle hybrid, was <u>derived</u> by agricultural scientists
A   B
from American, Russian and North African plants and <u>is able to survive</u> where
C
<u>fewer</u> rain falls.
 D

34. In 1995, President Clinton <u>doing</u> more to promote peace in <u>the</u> Middle East and
A   B
Ireland than <u>any</u> of his predecessors, yet <u>domestically</u> he remained unpopular.
C   D

35. <u>The</u> populace was <u>so terrified</u> of him that <u>however</u> he went he found the
 A   B   C
<u>villages</u> deserted of inhabitants and livestock.
   D

36. Encephalitis, an <u>inflammatory</u> of the brain, is also <u>being studied</u> by doctors at the
A   B
Chicago Research Center and rumors of <u>them</u> achieving an imminent breakthrough
C
<u>have been reported</u> by the press.
D

37. Almost one half <u>of</u> those <u>polled</u> in California said that they preferred to <u>vote on</u>
A   B   C
single issues rather than in normal party <u>election</u> because they didn't trust politicians.
D

GO ON TO THE NEXT PAGE

2 **2** **2** **2** **2** **2** **2** **2**

38. The discovery of the phonograph by Thomas Edison at the close of the century
      <u>   </u>
         A
    happened <u>as the result</u> of <u>an accident</u> in his work to <u>improve</u> the telegraph repeater.
              B   C   D

39. Unable to de-bug the newly installed system, the Californian Library Authority
    <u> </u>
     A
    <u>have reluctantly</u> decided that <u>their multi-million dollar</u> computer <u>will have to be</u>
          B   C   D
    scrapped.

40. The sextant was <u>an universal</u> instrument <u>used by</u> navigators to find locations <u>at sea</u>
                        A   B   C
    before <u>the advent</u> of satellite plotting.
                D

This is the end of Section 2.

If you finish in less than 25 minutes, check your work on Section 2 only.
Do NOT read or work on any other section of the test.

STOP STOP STOP STOP STOP STOP STOP

At the end of 25 minutes, go on to Section 3.
Use *exactly 55 minutes* to work on Section 3.

Section 2
Structure and
Written Expression

2

Time: 25 minutes (including the reading of the directions)
Now set your clock for 25 minutes.

This section is designed to measure your ability to recognize language that is appropriate for standard written English. There are two types of questions in this section, with special directions for each type.

Structure

Directions: Questions 1-15 are incomplete sentences. Beneath each sentence you will see four words or phrases, marked (A), (B), (C), and (D). Choose the <u>one</u> word or phrase that best completes the sentence. Then, on your answer sheet, find the number of the question and fill in the space that corresponds to the letter of the answer you have chosen. Fill in the space so that the letter inside the oval cannot be seen.

Example I   **Sample Answer**

The secretary of state -------   Ⓐ Ⓑ Ⓒ ●
on national TV tomorrow.

(A) he will be appearing
(B) appear
(C) who appears
(D) will be appearing

The sentence should read, "The secretary of state will be appearing on national TV tomorrow." Therefore, you should choose (D).

Example II   **Sample Answer**

How ------- after the flight?   Ⓐ Ⓑ ● Ⓓ

(A) the astronauts feel
(B) did feel the astronauts
(C) did the astronauts feel
(D) did the astronauts' feeling

The sentence should read, "How did the astronauts feel after the flight?" Therefore, you should choose (C).

Now begin work on the questions.

GO ON TO THE NEXT PAGE

② ② ② ② ② ② ② ②

1. At stake were major issues but --------
the rhetoric of global co-operation the
delegates were unable to make any
policy decisions.

   (A) even though
   (B) for all
   (C) since
   (D) only

2. When the currencies of developing
countries fluctuate, ------- changed
to dollars which widens the disparity
and is an additional handicap for the
countries to achieve stability.

   (A) money being
   (B) because money is
   (C) and money is
   (D) money is

3. As a uniquely-shaped cooking utensil,
the wok has been used in China for
thousands of years and has recently
------- popular in the US and
Europe.

   (A) became
   (B) become
   (C) becoming
   (D) being

4. The congressional report on the
various scandals ------- the ultimate
responsibility for the widespread
corruption and deceit on President
Reagan.

   (A) lays
   (B) layers
   (C) lay
   (D) laying

5. ------- of the Stamp Act in 1765 that
sparked the most resentment among
the American colonists and provoked
widespread opposition.

   (A) The introduction
   (B) It was the introduction
   (C) Before the introduction
   (D) During the introduction

6. In an effort to make the Constitution
both more accessible and understand-
able to the public, the House of
Representatives ------- the
publication of this pamphlet edition.

   (A) having authorization
   (B) authorizing
   (C) to authorize
   (D) have authorized

7. Unable to compete with America's
movie industry and shielded by
quotas, European television -------
dull, politically correct and obedient.

   (A) has become
   (B) become
   (C) becoming
   (D) have become

8. The prime purpose ------- to
determine whether the new Hughes
helicopter is suitably priced and
appropriate to the army's
requirements.

   (A) of the Defense Committee
   (B) for the Defense Committee
   (C) of the Defense Committee which
   is
   (D) of the Defense Committee is

GO ON TO THE NEXT PAGE

② ② ② ② ② ② ② ②

9. The new diet permits a wide range of even sweetened foods to be consumed, ------- bread, rice, pastries and dairy products.

(A) they include
(B) among them are
(C) including
(D) which included

10. ------- the worst urban violence since the partition of India, were blamed on religious strife between Hindus and Moslems.

(A) During the Bombay riots,
(B) The Bombay riots,
(C) The Bombay rioting,
(D) It was the Bombay riots,

11. Although defeated, ------- to scrap English as the official language of the US reflects the growing number of Spanish speaking Hispanic citizens.

(A) it was the proposal
(B) when the proposal
(C) the proposal
(D) while proposing

12. The catalytic converter not only allows more complete combustion thus causing less pollution -------

(A) but also produce more heat.
(B) and produces more heat as well.
(C) but produces more heat as well.
(D) but also producing more heat as well.

13. Scientists have attempted to increase the variability of wheat by inducing mutant strains but -------

(A) so far have met with great success.
(B) so far they have been meeting with little success.
(C) although so far have met with little success.
(D) so far have met with little success.

14. The Supreme Court is unlikely to uphold ------- against affirmative action but cross-party resentment is growing.

(A) that a Federal Court's decision
(B) a Federal Court's decision
(C) how a Federal Court's decision
(D) a Federal Court's deciding

15. The Gia is ------- makes of car produced in China that approaches the standards of a US vehicle.

(A) few
(B) the one
(C) one of the few
(D) only few

GO ON TO THE NEXT PAGE

② ② ② ② ② ② ② ②

Written Expression

Directions: In questions 16-40 each sentence has four underlined words or phrases. The four underlined parts of the sentence are marked (A), (B), (C), and (D). Identify the one underlined word or phrase that must be changed in order for the sentence to be correct. Then, on your answer sheet, find the number of the question and fill in the space that corresponds to the letter of the answer you have chosen.

Example I

Sample Answer

Ⓐ Ⓑ ● Ⓓ

Because of the storm all fifteen of the car failed
    A   B   C
to reach the check point.
    D

The sentence should read, "Because of the storm all fifteen of the cars failed to reach the check point." Therefore, you should choose (C).

Example II

Sample Answer

Ⓐ ● Ⓒ Ⓓ

The development of the attack helicopter begins at
          A   B
the end of last year and was completed within six
    C   D
months.

The sentence should read, "The development of the attack helicopter began at the end of last year and was completed within six months." Therefore, you should choose (B).

Now begin work on the questions.

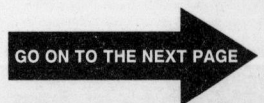

GO ON TO THE NEXT PAGE ➤

② ② ② ② ② ② ② ②

16. The most renowned composer of the fifteenth century was Josquin des Prèz who
    _____A_____   _____B_____
    was praised by Martin Luther and had received as many honors as Michelangelo.
                                   C   D

17. Since cadmium has been banned because of it's poisonous qualities, chemical
    _____A_____   _____B_____
    companies have been experimenting with tin as a substitute plastic stabilizer.
    _____C_____   _____D_____

18. Despite the technical and scientific innovations that have appeared since World
    ___A___   _____B_____   ____C____
    War Two, there have been little changes in the field of economics.
                       _____D_____

19. Because of the storm over Washington that day, many senators were absent but
    ___A___   ___B___
    everyone there gave their support to the bill.
                    ___C___ ___D___

20. When compared to the number of vehicles used by other similarly sized law
    __A__   __B__   ____C____
    enforcement agencies, three hundred cars seem extravagant.
                                        __D__

21. An African delegate reminded the conference that not only have half the world's
    _____A_____   _____B_____
    inhabitants never made a telephone call but also the general political atmosphere
               ___C___
    have obstructed progress.
    ___D___

22. The economic miracle is so fragile that a week in banking, as the Barings crash
                                    ___A___   ___B___
    revealed, are ample for even a major financial institution to slide from multi-million
              ___C___   ___D___
    dollar profit to bankruptcy.

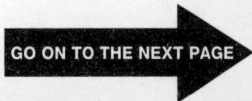

GO ON TO THE NEXT PAGE

2 2 2 2 2 2 2 2

23. The National Museum <u>announced the discovery</u> of sixty magnificently crafted
    A
    carousel animals <u>saying that</u> these treasures, each one a guaranteed original,
    B
    <u>have been hidden</u> from view <u>to two</u> generations.
    C   D

24. <u>Because of</u> the continuing tremors in <u>southern Japan</u> and mounting concern among
    A   B
    seismologists, from time to time <u>even the strongest</u> buildings are <u>being</u> evacuated as
    C   D
    a security precaution.

25. The Constitution <u>which has served</u> as the cornerstone of our nation's democracy
    A
    and <u>the principal guarantor</u> of freedom and equality as well as <u>being</u> a visible and
    B   C
    enduring <u>common bond</u> between the diverse peoples of America.
    D

26. At the age of twenty five, John Davis, <u>who by then</u> had already <u>been elected</u> to the
    A   B
    Senate, married Jennifer Irwin <u>who was</u> seven years older than <u>him</u>.
    C   D

27. After exhaustive tests, the scientists of the <u>Hopkins Clinic</u> were unable <u>to distinguish</u>
    A   B
    any <u>difference between</u> the three strains <u>of the HIV</u> samples.
    C   D

28. <u>Scientists</u> have expressed <u>concern</u> at the mounting level of toxic chemicals that have
    A   B
    <u>shown up</u> in the <u>protection</u> shell of various species of molluscs.
    C   D

29. Apple Mac, <u>the American</u> computer giant, <u>admitted that</u> a batch of substandard
    A   B
    <u>chips had been incorporated</u> into a limited number of appliances and recommended
    C
    the immediate return of <u>defective and faulty</u> machines.
    D

GO ON TO THE NEXT PAGE

18

2 2 2 2 2 2 2 2

30. Not until recent has it become clear, from newly disclosed archive material, how
    _____
    A
    close Kennedy took the world to the brink of a nuclear war in his efforts to persuade
                          _____   _____
                                   B   C
    Khrushchev to withdraw missiles from Cuba.
                         _____
                                   D

31. Natural gas, found in deposits all over the world beneath sea and land surfaces, offer
               _____   _____   _____
                      A   B   C
    the prime hope for an ecologically healthy environment.
                         _____
                                   D

32. Known as being fond of scotch, a good cigar and intelligent conversation, Churchill
    _____
       A
    had spent that year in New York being feted by wealthy party givers, but those
    _____   _____
               B   C
    relaxed, after-meal discourses molded his thoughts on the rise of Hitler.
                                   _____
                                            D

33. The Geneva conference concluded with a majority of the representatives accepting
    ___   _____
     A   B
    that much of the economic rescue packages would only provide temporary solutions.
         ____   _____
          C   D

34. The integrating process of European unions, many of which are closely affiliated,
    ___   _____
     A   B
    have already played a role in the increasing economic strengthening of Europe.
    ____   _____
      C   D

35. The Swedish police keep an updating computerized file on all citizens and even
                         _____
                               A
    visiting tourists, logging in everything from the value and nature of purchases made
                       _____   _____
                            B   C
    to travels abroad.
    _____
          D

36. Atomic powers, demonstrably a far from satisfactory means of generating
          _____   _____
            A   B
    electricity, remains the prime energy resource of France and a key research area of
             _____
                  C
    many developing countries for its prestige and defense spin-offs.
                                  _____
                                          D

GO ON TO THE NEXT PAGE

19

2 **2** **2** **2** **2** **2** **2** **2**

37. Janet Osgood, <u>delivered</u> by Dallas State Hospital doctors on July 3, 1994, weighed
                        A

     <u>less</u> than 1lb <u>at birth</u> and remains the <u>prematurest</u> baby ever to have survived.
      B   C   D

38. The average alcohol <u>content</u> of the best selling US beers <u>is below</u> the average of
                           A   B

     European beer <u>which is</u> more than seven <u>percents</u>.
                    C   D

39. The moral perspective <u>that makes</u> issues such as the death penalty, euthanasia and
                            A

     abortion <u>so</u> politically explosive <u>are to be discussed</u> on TV <u>by</u> all the candidates a
              B   C   D

     week before the election.

40. In the letter <u>signed by</u> the entire staff, <u>it was asked</u> when <u>would they receive</u> the
                    A   B   C

     promised pay <u>increase</u>.
                   D

This is the end of Section 2.

If you finish in less than 25 minutes, check your work on Section 2 only.
Do NOT read or work on any other section of the test.

(STOP) (STOP) (STOP) (STOP) (STOP) (STOP) (STOP)

At the end of 25 minutes, go on to Section 3.
Use *exactly 55 minutes* to work on Section 3.

Section 2
Structure and
Written Expression

2

Time: 25 minutes (including the reading of the directions)
Now set your clock for 25 minutes.

This section is designed to measure your ability to recognize language that is appropriate for standard written English. There are two types of questions in this section, with special directions for each type.

Structure

Directions: Questions 1-15 are incomplete sentences. Beneath each sentence you will see four words or phrases, marked (A), (B), (C), and (D). Choose the <u>one</u> word or phrase that best completes the sentence. Then, on your answer sheet, find the number of the question and fill in the space that corresponds to the letter of the answer you have chosen. Fill in the space so that the letter inside the oval cannot be seen.

Example I

The secretary of state ------- on national TV tomorrow.

(A) he will be appearing
(B) appear
(C) who appears
(D) will be appearing

Sample Answer

Ⓐ Ⓑ Ⓒ ●

The sentence should read, "The secretary of state will be appearing on national TV tomorrow." Therefore, you should choose (D).

Example II

How ------- after the flight?

(A) the astronauts feel
(B) did feel the astronauts
(C) did the astronauts feel
(D) did the astronauts' feeling

Sample Answer

Ⓐ Ⓑ ● Ⓓ

The sentence should read, "How did the astronauts feel after the flight?" Therefore, you should choose (C).

Now begin work on the questions.

GO ON TO THE NEXT PAGE

② ② ② ② ② ② ② ②

1. Made of a titanium alloy, the envisaged spaceship ------- less fuel to place the satellite into orbit.

   (A) require
   (B) requiring
   (C) requirement
   (D) would require

2. Closing the naval base, ------- argument as compelling today as it was two years ago, would deprive dedicated Navy reservists throughout our region of the opportunity to serve the nation.

   (A) an
   (B) it is an
   (C) that is an
   (D) of an

3. ------- origins of Greek tragedy are unclear is one of the reasons why, to this day, it remains controversial.

   (A) The
   (B) That the
   (C) Originally
   (D) Although the

4. The agreement signed by Arafat and Rabin in 1994 in Washington ------- a fragile peace in the region and won both men the Nobel Peace Prize.

   (A) establishing
   (B) was establishing
   (C) establishes
   (D) established

5. When ------- of electrons and volatile gasses in the chamber, an explosion takes place and the engine begins to function.

   (A) the simultaneous accumulations
   (B) simultaneously accumulate
   (C) there are simultaneous accumulations
   (D) simultaneously accumulating

6. The 39 delegates ------- the Constitution on September 17, 1787 expected the new charter to provide a permanent guarantee of the political liberties achieved in the Revolution.

   (A) signed
   (B) whom signed
   (C) which signed
   (D) who signed

7. The weasel uses the same burrow year after year, ------- new chambers each time.

   (A) and
   (B) enlarging it with
   (C) which is
   (D) enlargement

8. When ------- from the lower rock strata up to the periphery levels, a full-blown, spontaneous explosion may occur.

   (A) growing seepage
   (B) the growing seepage of gas
   (C) there is growing seepage of gas
   (D) are there growing seepage of gas

GO ON TO THE NEXT PAGE

2 2 2 2 2 2 2 2

9. The island of Alabara is the home of the world's largest and ------- of giant tortoise which on average reach a weight of 110lbs.

(A) a wild population
(B) it is the only wild population
(C) a wildest population
(D) only wild population

10. The bald eagle, one of two species of eagle found in the US, ------- on the US Seal of Office.

(A) it is enshrined
(B) is enshrined
(C) are enshrined
(D) which is enshrined

11. ------- eight million members of shooting and hunting associations, a clear majority of those polled opposed over-the-counter sales of handguns.

(A) More than
(B) Because more than
(C) There were more than
(D) Of the more than

12. In addition to having hired highly qualified lecturers, Mcgrath College ------- finest academic record of their history.

(A) have had a
(B) having had the
(C) has had the
(D) have had the

13. So fixed and widespread was the idea of the Earth being flat that ------- that the notion was accepted as false.

(A) it wasn't until after its circumnavigation
(B) it was its circumnavigation
(C) because of its circumnavigation
(D) it wasn't until after it's circumnavigation

14. Scientists believe that if a meteor as big as the one that caused the 400 mile wide Hudson Bay crater should strike us again, -------

(A) and the explosion would burn up the world's atmosphere.
(B) although the explosion would burn up the world's atmosphere.
(C) as the explosion would burn up the world's atmosphere.
(D) the explosion would burn up the world's atmosphere.

15. After passing through an unpleasant initial phase of flight caused by acceleration, -------

(A) a period of weightlessness is experienced by the astronauts.
(B) the astronauts experience a period of weightlessness.
(C) with the astronauts' experiencing a period of weightlessness.
(D) a period of weightlessness is being experienced by the astronauts.

GO ON TO THE NEXT PAGE

② ② ② ② ② ② ② ②

Written Expression

Directions: In questions 16-40 each sentence has four underlined words or phrases. The four underlined parts of the sentence are marked (A), (B), (C), and (D). Identify the <u>one</u> underlined word or phrase that must be changed in order for the sentence to be correct. Then, on your answer sheet, find the number of the question and fill in the space that corresponds to the letter of the answer you have chosen.

Example I

Sample Answer

Ⓐ Ⓑ ● Ⓓ

Because of the storm all fifteen of the car failed
    A   B   C
to reach the check point.
   D

The sentence should read, "Because of the storm all fifteen of the cars failed to reach the check point." Therefore, you should choose (C).

Example II

Sample Answer

Ⓐ ● Ⓒ Ⓓ

The development of the attack helicopter begins at
         A   B
the end of last year and was completed within six
  C   D
months.

The sentence should read, "The development of the attack helicopter began at the end of last year and was completed within six months." Therefore, you should choose (B).

Now begin work on the questions.

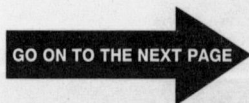

GO ON TO THE NEXT PAGE

24

② ② ② ② ② ② ② ②

16. Solzhenitsyn was awarded his 1970 Nobel literature prize in absentia because he
    <u>   </u>   <u>   </u>
         A   B
    feared the authorities would not let him to return to Russia.
    <u>   </u>   <u>   </u>
         C   D

17. Backache chronic is clearly one of the most common causes of long-term
    <u>   </u>   <u>   </u>
            A   B
    disability and absenteeism from work in the United States.
    <u>   </u>   <u>   </u>
            C   D

18. To do the work easier, a number of adaptations have been included such as
    <u>   </u>   <u>   </u>
        A   B
    automatic code reading and sorting machines but generally the postal service
                 <u>   </u>
                         C
    remains a labor intensive industry.
    <u>   </u>
        D

19. Until the invention of cable television, many people living in isolated regions could
          <u>   </u>   <u>   </u>
               A   B
    not get clearly reception on their TV sets.
    <u>   </u>   <u>   </u>
        C   D

20. Neither Dramamine, which is a potent drug against motion sickness, or extensive
                              <u>   </u>   <u> </u>
                                 A   B
    pre-flight training has been able to overcome the discomfort experienced by
    <u>   </u>
           C
    astronauts when re-entering the atmosphere.
    <u>   </u>
        D

21. All of the charter, including the new political liberties achieved by the Revolution
    <u>   </u>   <u>   </u>
          A   B
    and the personal rights of individuals, have been handed down from the founding
    <u>   </u>   <u>   </u>
             C   D
    fathers.

22. The US senate ordered that, consequent to the tragic disaster, all subsequent
                               <u>   </u>
                                   A
    discoveries of the field of genetics be reported immediately to the Senate Standing
    <u>   </u>   <u>   </u>
          B   C
    Committee for appraisal.
    <u>   </u>
        D

GO ON TO THE NEXT PAGE

② ② ② ② ② ② ② ②

23. Approved by the First Congress in 1789 and ratified by the states in 1791,
         ―――――
          A
     the first ten articles of the Constitution assure the basic liberties essential by a free
                                              ―――――――――――   ―――――――
          B   C   D
     and democratic society.

24. The report issued by the standing commission stated emphatically that
                ――――――
                  A
     supplementary funding was vital, as by the end of the next financial year all the
     ―――――――――――――
          B
     resources allocated by Congress will be exhausting.
     ―――――――――――――   ――――――――――
              C   D

25. By preventing any one of the three branches from acquiring political dominance
        ――――――――
             A
     over the others, these structural procedures unity while preserving a fundamental,
     ―――   ――――――――――――
      B   C
     although not always neat, separation of powers.
     ――――――
        D

26. Unlike the Washington Post, the New York Times is recognized by journalists and
     ――――
       A
     politicians alike for their sympathy towards moderate view points and this is
                     ―――   ―――――――
                      B   C
     reflected in the voting pattern of its readers.
                     ―――――――――――
                          D

27. The accident took place as the ship was sailing across the Subic Bay to the
                ―――――――――   ―――――――
                    A   B
     chemicals plant and the entire coast line was contaminated by toxic waste.
     ―――――――――   ――――――――――――――
         C   D

28. At the rear of the vehicle, to retain stability, is a micro-computerized sensing device
     ――――――――   ――――――――――――――――――
          A   B
     sends electrical impulses to the retractable pressure drums.
     ―――――   ―――――――――――
       C   D

GO ON TO THE NEXT PAGE

2 2 2 2 2 2 2 2

29. To clarify the situation the Mexican government confirmed that the conditions
    <u>   </u>
      A
    laid down in North American Free Trade Agreement would be adhered to
        B   C
    regardless of the fall in value of the peso.
                   D

30. Because of the break-in at the university, and despite vocal objections from the
            A   B
    student body, lectures were rescheduled and the entire class had to make the test
                          C   D
    again.

31. The purchase of the Panama Canal was advised because of a growing
            A   B
    understanding of its importance and because of a new global political awareness
          C   D
    on the part of the US government.

32. The current US Ambassador to France, Ms Harriman, is no stranger to the country
                                                   A
    as she once worked as a foreign correspondent based in Paris and she lived for a
       B   C   D
    time in the red light district of Pigalle.

33. At his retirement banquet, New York Commissioner Walters stressed that, although
      A
    much useful information could be gained from his experiences, a good amount of
       B   C
    the advise he had to give was outdated.
       D

34. The most space walks were logged up during this flight than in any other voyage
        A   B
    made by the Americans or the Russians and, of the three man crew, two
       C
    have since turned to religion.
        D

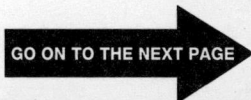

GO ON TO THE NEXT PAGE

② ② ② ② ② ② ② ②

35. Mike Tyson, the recently released boxer champion, is reported to have bigger
                          _____   _____
                                  A   B
    biceps, a four-inch wider chest, a far harder punch and faster reactions than he had
            _____
                     C
    before he was arrested.
    _____
              D

36. The two vehicles look alike yet beneath their hoods very different engines lie and
                        _____   _____
                            A   B
    just by listening to them tick over is it possible to tell them apart.
                        _____   _____
                               C   D

37. The Alsatian wild cat, which now thrive in the southern part of the Florida Swamps
                                 _____
                                      A
    region and is believed to have been first brought to the US as a domestic pet, feeds
    _____   _____
                 B   C
    mainly on fish scooped from the water with its paws.
                            _____
                                D

38. The backlash against affirmative discrimination, the favoring of companies
                 _____
                                  A
    headed and staffed by people from ethnic minorities, could decide the result of the
    _____   _____
              B   C
    next president election.
    _____
             D

39. The question of genetic engineering, although, has been considered far too complex
    _____   _____   _____
                 A   B   C
    and obscure for the general public to fully comprehend.
                         _____
                                      D

40. Jamestown, which excluding expeditionary locations was the first permanent
                                                        _____
                                                                 A
    English settlement in America, and it was founded in 1607.
    _____   ___   _____
             B   C   D

This is the end of Section 2.

If you finish in less than 25 minutes, check your work on Section 2 only.
Do NOT read or work on any other section of the test.

(STOP) (STOP) (STOP) (STOP) (STOP) (STOP) (STOP)

At the end of 25 minutes, go on to Section 3.

Use *exactly 55 minutes* to work on Section 3.

TEST FOUR

Section 2
Structure and
Written Expression

2

Time: 25 minutes (including the reading of the directions)
Now set your clock for 25 minutes.

This section is designed to measure your ability to recognize language that is appropriate for standard written English. There are two types of questions in this section, with special directions for each type.

Structure

Directions: Questions 1-15 are incomplete sentences. Beneath each sentence you will see four words or phrases, marked (A), (B), (C), and (D). Choose the <u>one</u> word or phrase that best completes the sentence. Then, on your answer sheet, find the number of the question and fill in the space that corresponds to the letter of the answer you have chosen. Fill in the space so that the letter inside the oval cannot be seen.

Example I

The secretary of state ------- on national TV tomorrow.

Sample Answer

Ⓐ Ⓑ Ⓒ ●

(A) he will be appearing
(B) appear
(C) who appears
(D) will be appearing

The sentence should read, "The secretary of state will be appearing on national TV tomorrow." Therefore, you should choose (D).

Example II

How ------- after the flight?

Sample Answer

Ⓐ Ⓑ ● Ⓓ

(A) the astronauts feel
(B) did feel the astronauts
(C) did the astronauts feel
(D) did the astronauts' feeling

The sentence should read, "How did the astronauts feel after the flight?" Therefore, you should choose (C).

Now begin work on the questions.

GO ON TO THE NEXT PAGE

2 2 2 2 2 2 2 2

1. Because of the harsh conditions, only during the summer months ------- accessible.

   (A) the area is
   (B) the area
   (C) has the area
   (D) is the area

2. Plato, ------- many Athenians, was strongly attracted to the teachings and personality of Socrates.

   (A) alike
   (B) while
   (C) as
   (D) like

3. The computer programs that have appeared since the appearance of the pentium chip ------- so sophisticated that applications undreamed of just a few years ago are now possible.

   (A) have become
   (B) will be
   (C) are being
   (D) becoming

4. The caterpillar larva, ------- throughout the world, has virtually no independent means of protecting itself from the attacks of predatory flies and wasps.

   (A) which are found
   (B) found
   (C) that are found
   (D) being found

5. Located on either side of the Bosphorus, -------

   (A) is the city of Istanbul bridging two continents.
   (B) the city of Istanbul bridges two continents.
   (C) two continents are bridged by the city of Istanbul.
   (D) the city of Istanbul which bridges two continents.

6. The debates of the state ratification conventions of 1787 and 1788 ------- the need to provide amendments to the basic framework drafted in Philadelphia.

   (A) made clear
   (B) they make clear
   (C) making clear
   (D) makes clear

7. ------- world-wide for his role of the ragged vagabond, Charlie Chaplin was for a long time persecuted by the US government for his beliefs.

   (A) He is loved
   (B) To love
   (C) He loves
   (D) Though loved

8. Research has shown that exposure to asbestos causes ------- health problems.

   (A) much serious
   (B) serious
   (C) often seriously
   (D) many serious often

GO ON TO THE NEXT PAGE

② ② ② ② ② ② ② ②

9. The mummies of the Chinchorro,
------- fisher folk, were discovered
in 1960 along the coasts of Peru and
Chile.

(A) who were being prehistoric
(B) prehistoric
(C) are prehistoric
(D) its prehistoric

10. ------- in that part of Alaska, the
entire oil terminal had to be built
from scratch.

(A) Being no facilities
(B) There were no facilities
(C) Because there was no facilities
(D) Since there were no facilities

11. No single individual has done more
to better the situation of these
impoverished people -------

(A) then Mother Theresa.
(B) it being Mother Theresa.
(C) she was Mother Theresa.
(D) than Mother Theresa.

12. ------- from pro football, OJ Simpson
had been ranked with Jim Brown as
the greatest running back of all time.

(A) Before he is retiring
(B) He retired
(C) As he retired
(D) Before his retirement

13. First and foremost among America's
nineteenth century popular novelists
------- who thrilled readers with his
tales of Mississippi river folk.

(A) Mark Twain came
(B) is coming Mark Twain
(C) comes Mark Twain
(D) Mark Twain was coming

14. Between May and September the US
marines obtained signals to chart the
locations of the dolphins using
------- under their hide.

(A) implanted transmitters
(B) implanted in transmitters
(C) transmitters implanted
(D) transmitters were implanted

15. ------- to sting has been a subject
of research by biologists at the
university.

(A) What antagonizes the wasp
(B) That antagonizes the wasp
(C) Although the wasp is
antagonized
(D) It is the antagonization of the
wasp

GO ON TO THE NEXT PAGE

2 2 2 2 2 2 2 2

Written Expression

Directions: In questions 16-40 each sentence has four underlined words or phrases. The four underlined parts of the sentence are marked (A), (B), (C), and (D). Identify the one underlined word or phrase that must be changed in order for the sentence to be correct. Then, on your answer sheet, find the number of the question and fill in the space that corresponds to the letter of the answer you have chosen.

Example I

Sample Answer

Ⓐ Ⓑ ● Ⓓ

Because of the storm all fifteen of the car failed
    A   B   C
to reach the check point.
  D

The sentence should read, "Because of the storm all fifteen of the cars failed to reach the check point." Therefore, you should choose (C).

Example II

Sample Answer

Ⓐ ● Ⓒ Ⓓ

The development of the attack helicopter begins at
             A   B
the end of last year and was completed within six
    C   D
months.

The sentence should read, "The development of the attack helicopter began at the end of last year and was completed within six months." Therefore, you should choose (B).

Now begin work on the questions.

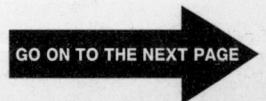

GO ON TO THE NEXT PAGE

② ② ② ② ② ② ② ②

16. Whether or not the GATT talks are successful depends to the will of all the
    <u>   </u>   <u>   </u>
                 A   B
    participating parties and <u>full compliance</u> with any resolutions that <u>are reached</u>.
                            C   D

17. <u>The</u> pioneers of 'test tube baby' births, <u>when the experiments first began in 1971</u>,
     A   B
    <u>they were forced to cancel</u> their plans <u>because of</u> the controversy that erupted.
               C   D

18. <u>The</u> Chicago transport system, <u>redesigned and modernized in 1992</u>, now <u>carries</u>
     A   B   C
    more than a million passengers a day <u>swiftly and quickly</u> to their destinations.
                                                 D

19. Utility costs have <u>risen</u> so rapidly <u>during</u> the last few years that a good many
                        A   B
    <u>lower-income</u> families have found themselves unable to pay <u>their bills</u>.
          C   D

20. <u>Although</u> CBS news programs attract bigger audiences than NBC, <u>the latter</u>
     A   B
    company continues <u>to receive</u> high ratings for <u>its</u> entertainment programs.
                           C   D

21. The museum staff <u>acknowledges</u> the efforts of <u>many archaeologists</u> and the
                       A   B
    generosity of World Imports, <u>whose workmen</u> discovered the collection, in their
                                       C
    annual report <u>to be issued</u> next month.
                        D

22. During his introductory speech <u>with the other members of the Senate</u>, Governor
        A   B
    Michaels <u>had claimed</u> attempts <u>had been made</u> to sabotage his campaign.
                 C   D

23. The McHale Amendment <u>seeks to define</u> the legal determination of a frivolous
                         A
    complaint that <u>must be present</u> for a court to dismiss a claim and <u>award</u> legal costs
                       B   C
    <u>from a defendant</u>.
          D

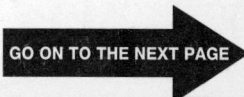

GO ON TO THE NEXT PAGE ▶

2 2 2 2 2 2 2 2

24. At a press conference held in his fifteenth-floor penthouse last night, the new
      —————————— A   —————————— B
    champion's arm was bandaged and he explained that he was bit by a poisonous
                   ———————— C   ———— D
    snake.

25. Although developing over two centuries ago, the Constitution continues to perform
    ——————— A
    its essential function despite the dramatic societal, technological, economic, and
    — B   ———— C
    political changes in the United States over the past two centuries.
                          —————————— D

26. Madras is the third largest city of the sub-continent which is exceeded in size only
                  ———— A   ———— B   ———— C   ———— D
    by the cities of Delhi and Bombay.

27. Carl Lewis, the world record smashing, gold medal winning, Olympic sprinter,
                                           ————————————— A
    had broke his leg as a teenager and been warned by several medical experts that he
    ———— B   ———— C
    would never run again.
    ———————— D

28. Washington has long been considered the murder capital of the world yet over the
              —————————————— A   ————————— B
    last year the number of fatalities have fallen thanks to better policing and the
                                       ———— C   ———— D
    restricted sales of weapons.

29. Because of its gratuitous violence and explicit sex content, the controller of the TV
    ——————— A   ————————— B
    station has decided to soon cancel the crime series in the near future.
           ———— C   ———— D

30. Traditionally most funerals were held on the weekend people were free from work,
                   ———————— A   ————————— B
    but even then they first had to obtain permission to attend from their overseers.
                            ———————————— C   ———— D

GO ON TO THE NEXT PAGE

2 2 2 2 2 2 2 2

31. None of the two options facing the bank, sacking their rogue dealer or supporting
    __A__   __B__
    him further, was satisfactory and their equivocating eventually cost them millions.
    __C__   __D__

32. Getty generally avoided meeting his staff but made an exception when he invited
    _____A_____   __B__
    Harris to his ranch because of his years of dedicated service and stock market
    __C__
    dealings had gained millions for the reclusive billionaire.
    __D__

33. If the Reds are able to maintain the same extraordinary batting average for the rest
    __A__
    of the season there maybe a slim chance that they'll reach the playoffs this coming
    __B__   __C__   __D__
    June.

34. Although under orthodox Islamic rule a man is permitted to have four wifes, abuses
    __A__   __B__
    are rare as he is obliged to care for them equally and becomes the object of moral
    __C__   __D__
    scrutiny by his peers.

35. There is a rare species of frog native to North America which hibernates encased in
    __A__   __B__
    ice with its blood being freezing but then awakens each spring when the ice melts.
    __C__   __D__

36. The circles are believed to have been formed by the Incas' cultivation of thousands
    __A__   __B__
    of square miles of coca which many anthropologists believe were force fed to
    __C__   __D__
    workers.

37. A surprising small number of champion American race horses, including Kentucky
    __A__   __B__
    Derby winners, have been able to match such successes when racing in Europe.
    __C__   __D__

GO ON TO THE NEXT PAGE

② ② ② ② ② ② ② ②

38. The most controversial element of Roosevelt's New Deal program, adopted to
    <u>A</u>   <u>B</u>
    provide work during the Great Depression, was the Federal Arts Project to give
                                                      <u>C</u>
    employings to artists.
    <u>D</u>

39. The consequences of cloud seeding, a sole technique to artificially cause
    <u>A</u>   <u>B</u>
    precipitation, are now being seriously debated by Israeli environmental scientists.
    <u>C</u>   <u>D</u>

40. Reading between the lines, the report made clear to all who read it was the amount
    <u>A</u>   <u>B</u>   <u>C</u>
    of mis-information that had been released over the years.
                         <u>D</u>

This is the end of Section 2.

If you finish in less than 25 minutes, check your work on Section 2 only.
Do NOT read or work on any other section of the test.

STOP STOP STOP **STOP** STOP STOP STOP

At the end of 25 minutes, go on to Section 3.
Use *exactly 55 minutes* to work on Section 3.

Section 2
Structure and
Written Expression

2

Time: 25 minutes (including the reading of the directions)
Now set your clock for 25 minutes.

This section is designed to measure your ability to recognize language that is appropriate for standard written English. There are two types of questions in this section, with special directions for each type.

Structure

Directions: Questions 1-15 are incomplete sentences. Beneath each sentence you will see four words or phrases, marked (A), (B), (C), and (D). Choose the <u>one</u> word or phrase that best completes the sentence. Then, on your answer sheet, find the number of the question and fill in the space that corresponds to the letter of the answer you have chosen. Fill in the space so that the letter inside the oval cannot be seen.

Example I

The secretary of state ------- on national TV tomorrow.

Sample Answer

Ⓐ Ⓑ Ⓒ ●

(A) he will be appearing
(B) appear
(C) who appears
(D) will be appearing

The sentence should read, "The secretary of state will be appearing on national TV tomorrow." Therefore, you should choose (D).

Example II

How ------- after the flight?

Sample Answer

Ⓐ Ⓑ ● Ⓓ

(A) the astronauts feel
(B) did feel the astronauts
(C) did the astronauts feel
(D) did the astronauts' feeling

The sentence should read, "How did the astronauts feel after the flight?" Therefore, you should choose (C).

Now begin work on the questions.

GO ON TO THE NEXT PAGE

1. The Nevada gold rush began in 1859 ------- within weeks the area was invaded by prospectors from the East.

   (A) because
   (B) that
   (C) and
   (D) while

2. Jacob Lawrence ------- in the New York district of Harlem when it was undergoing a flowering of black culture called the "Harlem Renaissance."

   (A) born
   (B) who was born
   (C) was born
   (D) being born

3. Recent events in what was once Yugoslavia have brought into question the purpose and ------- of the United Nations as an organization to maintain peace in the world.

   (A) are generally effective
   (B) to be generally effective
   (C) general effectiveness
   (D) being generally effective

4. Only once over the past few years ------- so overwhelmingly to oppose the will of the presidency.

   (A) the Senate has voted
   (B) the Senate will vote
   (C) has the Senate voted
   (D) the Senate voted

5. ------- our recent celebration of the bicentennial of the Bill of Rights, it is particularly appropriate that the House of Representatives issues this pamphlet edition of the Constitution.

   (A) Depending on
   (B) Only due to
   (C) In light of
   (D) Merely

6. Unlike its predecessor, which only accepted Apple software, ------- to Microsoft and DOS programmes.

   (A) and switched the new Apple Power
   (B) switching the new Apple Power
   (C) is switching the new Apple Power
   (D) the new Apple Power can be switched

7. The dehydrated milk was sent in heat proof packs ------- ideal for storage in the UNICEF warehouse.

   (A) that making them
   (B) that is
   (C) which made it
   (D) and its

8. The Committee for Un-American Activities was empowered not only to summons individuals for questioning ------- to detain them in a specially designated detention center.

   (A) and to
   (B) but occasionally
   (C) occasionally
   (D) and also

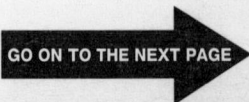
GO ON TO THE NEXT PAGE

② ② ② ② ② ② ② ②

9. In Bombay, ------- can run as high as in New York, real estate is an especially coveted commodity.

   (A) where land prices
   (B) land prices
   (C) who's land prices
   (D) because of land prices

10. The resignation of the president was a shock to government aides and party supporters ------- by the vice president who knew of the illness.

    (A) and also had been expected
    (B) which is expected
    (C) expected
    (D) but had been expected

11. Einstein explained that the reason why he had only one bar of soap to shave, wash and shampoo his hair with was that more soap products ------- too complicated.

    (A) had been
    (B) is
    (C) are being
    (D) would have been

12. Supporters of nuclear energy to produce electricity ------- three arguments, two of them economic and the third political.

    (A) while usually quoting
    (B) usually quoting
    (C) who usually quote
    (D) usually quote

13. A major reason for a company ------- a health and pension plan is that in the long term their investment is recouped by lower absenteeism.

    (A) to initiate and maintaining
    (B) to initiate and maintain
    (C) which initiate and maintain
    (D) that initiating and maintaining

14. ------- last October, the Euro Palace is in some ways reminiscent of the White House.

    (A) Finishes
    (B) Finished
    (C) Finishing
    (D) To finish

15. With regard to the longevity of stars, ------- the longer the life span.

    (A) the slower is the development
    (B) when development is slow
    (C) the slower the development
    (D) slowing development

GO ON TO THE NEXT PAGE

② ② ② ② ② ② ② ②

Written Expression

Directions: In questions 16-40 each sentence has four underlined words or phrases. The four underlined parts of the sentence are marked (A), (B), (C), and (D). Identify the one underlined word or phrase that must be changed in order for the sentence to be correct. Then, on your answer sheet, find the number of the question and fill in the space that corresponds to the letter of the answer you have chosen.

Example I

Sample Answer

Ⓐ Ⓑ ● Ⓓ

Because of the storm all fifteen of the car failed
_____   ___   ___
        A   B   C
to reach the check point.
___
  D

The sentence should read, "Because of the storm all fifteen of the cars failed to reach the check point." Therefore, you should choose (C).

Example II

Sample Answer

Ⓐ ● Ⓒ Ⓓ

The development of the attack helicopter begins at
_____   _____
        A   B
the end of last year and was completed within six
___   _____
  C   D
months.

The sentence should read, "The development of the attack helicopter began at the end of last year and was completed within six months." Therefore, you should choose (B).

Now begin work on the questions.

GO ON TO THE NEXT PAGE

2 2 2 2 2 2 2 2

16. Plans by a private company to offer genetic tests for inheriting disease direct to the
    <u>   </u>   A   B
    public were criticized by scientists as controversial and premature.
          <u>   </u>   C   <u>   </u>
                                                           D

17. President Clinton, together with the leaders and officials of thirteen Latin
                    <u>   </u>   <u>   </u>
                         A   B
    American countries, have begun the Miami summit conference with an optimistic
                    <u>   </u>
                         C
    assessment of the region's future.
    <u>   </u>
         D

18. A smallest deviation from the formulae could create substantial problems in the
    <u></u>   <u>   </u>
    A   B
    latter phases of production of this highly complex and delicate material.
    <u></u>   <u>   </u>
    C   D

19. Despite the economic slump, the number of students who have applied for loans and
                <u>   </u>   <u>   </u> <u>   </u>
                     A   B   C
    scholarships have remained constant.
    <u>   </u>
                     D

20. Rejecting the Conyers motion, the Committee on the Judiciary displays little
    <u>   </u>   <u>   </u>   <u>   </u>
         A   B   C
    evidence of research and practical on-site investigation to support their findings.
                                        <u>   </u>
                                              D

21. As a result of the plane crash, the number of restoration experts who used wood
    <u>   </u>   <u>   </u>
         A   B
    carvers' inscriptions to identify twelve of the animals are now down to six.
    <u>   </u>   <u>   </u>
         C   D

22. Immediate access in the work of colleagues and a "virtual" library of millions of
                    <u>   </u>   <u>   </u>
                         A   B
    volumes and thousands of papers afford academics an opportunity to utilize a body
                                    <u>   </u>   <u>   </u>
                                              C   D
    of knowledge heretofore unthinkable.

23. The significance of the network, in particular the ability to move vast amounts of
        <u>   </u>   <u>   </u>
             A   B
    information quickly in great distances, has yet to be fully appreciated.
                <u>   </u>   <u>   </u>
                     C   D

GO ON TO THE NEXT PAGE

2 **2** **2** **2** **2** **2** **2** **2**

24. Profits from <u>trading in futures</u> and derivatives <u>have become</u> the most rewarding
    A B
    sector <u>in the banking industry</u> since this field of finance <u>is becoming</u> apparent.
    C D

25. Camus <u>arrived back</u> at his Paris home <u>to find</u> the manuscript on the doorstep and
    A B
    <u>realized</u> it must have been <u>them</u> who had left the message.
    C D

26. When an <u>Internet</u> user decides to <u>switch to another network</u> to access from a
    A B
    wider <u>range of information</u>, <u>they</u> should be prepared to make mistakes.
    C D

27. <u>Beside</u> three properties <u>in Washington</u> and a private Caribbean island, several secret
    A B
    Swiss bank accounts <u>holding millions of dollars</u> were <u>uncovered by</u> the FBI.
    C D

28. Geothermal scientists <u>believe there is hot</u> enough water <u>beneath the US</u> to fill 20
    A B
    percent of <u>its</u> energy <u>requirements</u> for a hundred years.
    C D

29. <u>Merely</u> by adding catalytic filters and making a <u>few minor adjustments</u> to the
    A B
    firing mechanism it is possible to ensure that <u>virtually</u> any engine runs efficiently
    C
    <u>without polluting</u> the atmosphere.
    D

30. The <u>disciplined</u> mind and artistic courage described by critics as the essence
    A
    of <u>Parker's talent</u> is not really <u>on display</u> at this exhibition and really <u>are</u>
    B C
    more <u>discernible</u> at his private New York gallery.
    D

GO ON TO THE NEXT PAGE

2 2 2 2 2 2 2 2

31. Both Flemish and French are spoken in the area but the former is used most and
    <u> </u>   A   B

    is still generally <u>regarded as</u> an indication of a socially and <u>culturally deprived</u>
                          C   D

    background.

32. Although the trade imbalance <u>between</u> the US and Japan <u>persists</u>, the trade talks
                                        A   B

    have <u>failed to</u> attract the financial journalists <u>whom</u> normally cover such fields.
            C   D

33. Virtually all academic studies <u>bring with them</u> a legacy of male dominated thinking
                                            A

    but modern <u>anthropology</u>, because of the <u>undeniable importance</u> of women to the
                        B   C

    history <u>of the human race</u>, are being forced to rectify this fault.
                        D

34. Boris Akhalin, a foremost champion chess player who <u>insisted on</u> carrying his cat
                                                      A

    instead of a passport <u>wherever</u> he traveled, <u>he</u> became the Russian national
                              B   C

    champion <u>while still</u> a teenager.
               D

35. The <u>Washington</u> Causeway <u>which became</u> famous as <u>the site of</u> an accident
       A   B   C

    involving Ted Kennedy and a secretary who <u>was drowned</u> in suspicious
                                                      D

    circumstances.

36. The Patriot missile was <u>too</u> spectacularly inefficient <u>that</u> the Senate Weapons
                               A   B

    Procurement Committee <u>came near</u> to indicting <u>its makers</u> for fraud.
                             C   D

GO ON TO THE NEXT PAGE

2 2 2 2 2 2 2 2

37. The figures used by the supporters of the Wellington Amendment limiting tax
    —A—   ————B————   C
    rebates on corporate profits were provided by statistics John Freeham of Harvard
                                       ————D————
    University.

38. The successful extraction of the protein gamma globulin from blood plasma
    ———————A———————   ————B————
    requires crystallization, separation and also ultra-violet light is necessary.
    ——————————C——————————   ——————————D——————————

39. A binary star is actually a pair of stars that is held together by the force of gravity
            ————A————   —B—   —————C—————
    and seen from Earth as a single entity.
                            ———————D———————

40. Very little is known about the origins of the HIV virus except that it is a fairly recent
    —A—   ——————B——————
    development is a major obstacle for those seeking its cure.
    ——————C——————   ——D——

This is the end of Section 2.

If you finish in less than 25 minutes, check your work on Section 2 only.
Do NOT read or work on any other section of the test.

STOP STOP STOP STOP STOP STOP STOP

At the end of 25 minutes, go on to Section 3.

Use *exactly 55 minutes* to work on Section 3.

TEST SIX

Section 2
Structure and
Written Expression

2

Time: 25 minutes (including the reading of the directions)
Now set your clock for 25 minutes.

This section is designed to measure your ability to recognize language that is appropriate for standard written English. There are two types of questions in this section, with special directions for each type.

Structure

Directions: Questions 1-15 are incomplete sentences. Beneath each sentence you will see four words or phrases, marked (A), (B), (C), and (D). Choose the <u>one</u> word or phrase that best completes the sentence. Then, on your answer sheet, find the number of the question and fill in the space that corresponds to the letter of the answer you have chosen. Fill in the space so that the letter inside the oval cannot be seen.

Example I   **Sample Answer**

The secretary of state -------   Ⓐ Ⓑ Ⓒ ●
on national TV tomorrow.

(A) he will be appearing
(B) appear
(C) who appears
(D) will be appearing

The sentence should read, "The secretary of state will be appearing on national TV tomorrow." Therefore, you should choose (D).

Example II   **Sample Answer**

How ------- after the flight?   Ⓐ Ⓑ ● Ⓓ

(A) the astronauts feel
(B) did feel the astronauts
(C) did the astronauts feel
(D) did the astronauts' feeling

The sentence should read, "How did the astronauts feel after the flight?" Therefore, you should choose (C).

Now begin work on the questions.

GO ON TO THE NEXT PAGE ➡

②②②②②②②

1. In tomorrow's society, the traditional role of men will disappear ------- their capacity for aggression and instinct to dominate women will be redundant.

    (A) because of
    (B) depends on
    (C) as
    (D) but as

2. The chameleon's capacity to change color and camouflage itself is being studied by scientists ------- to the creation of a new uniform.

    (A) in order
    (B) with a view
    (C) trying to make
    (D) in the hope

3. ------- the financial success of World Cup '94, compared to basket ball and American football, soccer remains a minority sports activity.

    (A) In addition to
    (B) Despite
    (C) Although
    (D) Because of

4. ------- were the astronauts that the training period was shortened by several weeks.

    (A) Enthusiastically
    (B) So enthusiastic
    (C) Although enthusiastic
    (D) However enthusiastic

5. ------- they wisely built in a flexibility to accommodate change so that a living instrument of government could be passed down to succeeding generations.

    (A) In order to
    (B) Although
    (C) Because
    (D) By so doing,

6. In brief, the article claimed ------- American Indians are the descendants of Turkic nomads who reached the continent by crossing the Bering Straits.

    (A) of
    (B) that the
    (C) if
    (D) how the

7. ------- the conclusion of the war, Baker was able to return to his career as a union lawyer and became a congressional representative.

    (A) It was
    (B) On
    (C) In addition to the
    (D) With

8. According to statistical analysis of the findings, the harder the impact of the bullet -------

    (A) the smaller the entry wound become.
    (B) and the smaller the entry wound.
    (C) but the smaller is the entry wound.
    (D) the smaller the entry wound.

GO ON TO THE NEXT PAGE

② ② ② ② ② ② ② ②

9. ------- as the first Postmaster General, worked tirelessly to improve the efficiency of the postal service.

    (A) It was Benjamin Franklin,
    (B) Being Benjamin Franklin,
    (C) While Benjamin Franklin,
    (D) Benjamin Franklin,

10. To cater for American tastes, ------- soccer matches of four quarters instead of two halves.

    (A) junior leagues are experimenting on
    (B) junior leagues are experimenting with
    (C) junior leagues will be experimenting
    (D) as junior leagues are experimenting at

11. The Bay Bridge though longer than the Golden Gate Bridge ------- less well known to tourists visiting San Francisco.

    (A) is
    (B) but is
    (C) being
    (D) have been

12. While some people condemn television as a negative influence on children, ------- contribution to children's education.

    (A) others praise it to its
    (B) others praise it for it's
    (C) but others praise it for its
    (D) others praise it for its

13. The terrorist nerve gas attack on the Tokyo subway is a nightmare come true, ------- vulnerable society is to weapons of mass destruction.

    (A) which reveal how
    (B) it reveals how
    (C) and revealing how
    (D) revealing how

14. Forced random blood testing, ------- as the incident that sparked the rioting, has become the norm throughout the prison system.

    (A) such
    (B) similar
    (C) like
    (D) same

15. In none of the reports of the Kurdish-Turkish war which has already incurred thousands of fatalities ------- how the US OPC troops can be calmly based in the midst of a war zone.

    (A) is surprise expressed that
    (B) has surprisingly expressed
    (C) have surprises been expressed at
    (D) has surprise been expressed at

GO ON TO THE NEXT PAGE

② ② ② ② ② ② ②

Written Expression

Directions: In questions 16-40 each sentence has four underlined words or phrases. The four underlined parts of the sentence are marked (A), (B), (C), and (D). Identify the one underlined word or phrase that must be changed in order for the sentence to be correct. Then, on your answer sheet, find the number of the question and fill in the space that corresponds to the letter of the answer you have chosen.

Example I

Sample Answer

Ⓐ Ⓑ ● Ⓓ

Because of the storm all fifteen of the car failed
_____   _____
   A   B   C
to reach the check point.
_____
   D

The sentence should read, "Because of the storm all fifteen of the cars failed to reach the check point." Therefore, you should choose (C).

Example II

Sample Answer

Ⓐ ● Ⓒ Ⓓ

The development of the attack helicopter begins at
   _____   _____
          A   B
the end of last year and was completed within six
   ____   _____
    C   D
months.

The sentence should read, "The development of the attack helicopter began at the end of last year and was completed within six months." Therefore, you should choose (B).

Now begin work on the questions.

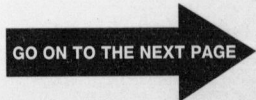

GO ON TO THE NEXT PAGE →

② ② ② ② ② ② ②

16. The Bill of Rights was conceived out of humanitarian considerations and
    <u>A</u>   <u>B</u>
    specifically appends to the Constitution to protect the rights of individuals.
    <u>C</u>   <u>D</u>

17. Alike other cars, the GM Electrica relies on a weighty, speed restricting battery
    <u>A</u>   <u>B</u>
    pack but has the advantage of being environmentally friendly.
    <u>C</u>   <u>D</u>

18. The Empire State Building and other skyscrapers which raise above the skyline of
    <u>A</u>   <u>B</u>
    New York are an important tourist attraction as well as providing acres of office
    <u>C</u>   <u>D</u>
    space.

19. Under the GATT agreement, a subsidized loan along with tax rebates were accepted
    <u>A</u>   <u>B</u>
    as the prime means to stimulate economic recovery.
    <u>C</u>   <u>D</u>

20. Technology is dividing the world into those capable of understanding and
    <u>A</u>
    mastering it and ordinary, common people who, regardless of their race and culture,
    <u>B</u>   <u>C</u>
    are condemned to be second class citizens.
    <u>D</u>

21. The New Jersey detectives disappointed the newsmen by saying that neither the
    <u>A</u>   <u>B</u>
    hundreds of gold bars nor the large amount of money recovered are being stored in
    <u>C</u>   <u>D</u>
    the station.

22. The Natick Lab, with its current 1,200 scientific and technical workers, is a state-of-
    <u>A</u>   <u>B</u>
    the-art army facility whose mission is to develop advanced equipment and rations
    <u>C</u>
    not only for the army but for other branches of the armed forces.
    <u>D</u>

GO ON TO THE NEXT PAGE

2 2 2 2 2 2 2 2

23. An examination <u>of the effects</u> produced by the new serum <u>indicate</u> that it is <u>not so</u>
                   A   B   C
<u>efficient</u> as the old class B serum.
  D

24. Despite the efforts of <u>the steering committee</u>, the cost of <u>the modernization</u>, research
                                A   B
and <u>development have risen</u> dramatically <u>over</u> the last five years.
              C   D

25. On the same day in 1492 that Columbus <u>set out and embarked</u> on his voyage to
                                                      A
<u>discover</u> the New World, Pirri Reis, <u>an Ottoman admiral</u>, began a rescue operation
  B   C
of thousands of <u>Spanish Jews from the Inquisition</u>.
                         D

26. <u>Regarding</u> as a symbol <u>for African American</u> advancement, OJ Simpson's career
    A   B
as <u>a sportsman</u> and TV personality <u>makes</u> his trial for murder <u>all the more</u>
                             C   D
extraordinary.

27. <u>The mosquito</u>, one of the <u>most resilient</u> creatures in the world, are to <u>be found</u> even
     A   B   C
within the Arctic and Antarctic circles and dates back millions <u>of years before the</u>
                                                                         D
appearance of man.

28. Of the three choices that were recommended to Washington at the meeting and
  A
had the <u>general support</u> of his war cabinet, the first <u>amounted to</u> political suicide
               B   C
and <u>the latter spelt</u> economic disaster.
           D

GO ON TO THE NEXT PAGE

2 **2** **2** **2** **2** **2** **2** **2**

29. To combat growing hyper-inflation in Russia and other East European countries,
    <u>A</u>   <u>B</u>
    there were many proposals <u>put forward</u> but so far none of those <u>done</u> seem to really
                              C   D
    address the basic issues.

30. The weather service announced that <u>because</u> of deteriorating conditions,
                                        A
    <u>brought about</u> by Hurricane Charlie, <u>farther</u> weather reports <u>would be given</u> at
           B   C   D
    hourly intervals.

31. <u>Giving</u> that throughout the world private non-governmental organizations, <u>such as</u>
        A   B
    Oxfam, are <u>more</u> efficient and successful in the field than the UN, many people are
               C
    beginning to question the role of governments in <u>international affairs</u>.
                                                     D

32. <u>Among</u> an array of great North American <u>writer</u>, Joseph Heller is <u>notable</u> for his
        A   B   C
    prolific output and literary ambitions, always <u>striving</u> to perfect his talent and style.
                                                   D

33. The speed <u>with which</u> East European countries <u>have adapted</u> to the free market has
               A   B
    astonished many economists but long term prosperity, <u>they claim</u>, is <u>dependent to</u>
                                                          C   D
    rapid modernization of old industries.

34. John Quincy Adams, <u>who served</u> as the 6th US president <u>from 1825 to 1829</u>, was
                        A   B
    known for his statesmanship, and <u>diplomacy</u> and dedication <u>to justice</u>.
                                     C   D

35. In the US, <u>the level</u> of illiteracy <u>is growing</u> over the past ten years and now some
                A   B
    <u>educationalists maintain</u> that it has reached <u>more than 20 percent</u>.
                C   D

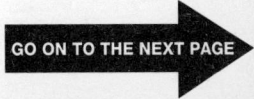

GO ON TO THE NEXT PAGE

② ② ② ② ② ② ② ②

36. When winter descends to the bulk of North America, the climate of Florida remains
     A   B   C   D
mild and pleasant.

37. Pure luck, rather than the technological advantages derived from world class firms,
           A   B
universities, and laboratories, have given the US its dominant role
                                          C
in global economics.
      D

38. The largest problem people face using a network is grasping the new possibilities
          A   B
available by them, as even seasoned users find themselves surprised at discovering a
      C   D
new service or application.

39. Unlike the situation in North America and Europe, the number of female AIDS
     A
sufferers to be found in East Africa and several areas of West Africa are statistically
       B   C
higher than male victims.
     D

40. Of the two Lincoln brothers, John had been the most successful in school but Paul
  A   B   C
had been taller than him.
     D

This is the end of Section 2.

If you finish in less than 25 minutes, check your work on Section 2 only.
Do NOT read or work on any other section of the test.

STOP STOP STOP **STOP** STOP STOP STOP

At the end of 25 minutes, go on to Section 3.
Use *exactly 55 minutes* to work on Section 3.

Section 2
Structure and
Written Expression

2

Time: 25 minutes (including the reading of the directions)
Now set your clock for 25 minutes.

This section is designed to measure your ability to recognize language that is appropriate for standard written English. There are two types of questions in this section, with special directions for each type.

Structure

Directions: Questions 1-15 are incomplete sentences. Beneath each sentence you will see four words or phrases, marked (A), (B), (C), and (D). Choose the <u>one</u> word or phrase that best completes the sentence. Then, on your answer sheet, find the number of the question and fill in the space that corresponds to the letter of the answer you have chosen. Fill in the space so that the letter inside the oval cannot be seen.

Example I   **Sample Answer**

The secretary of state -------   Ⓐ Ⓑ Ⓒ ●
on national TV tomorrow.

(A) he will be appearing
(B) appear
(C) who appears
(D) will be appearing

The sentence should read, "The secretary of state will be appearing on national TV tomorrow." Therefore, you should choose (D).

Example II   **Sample Answer**

How ------- after the flight?   Ⓐ Ⓑ ● Ⓓ

(A) the astronauts feel
(B) did feel the astronauts
(C) did the astronauts feel
(D) did the astronauts' feeling

The sentence should read, "How did the astronauts feel after the flight?" Therefore, you should choose (C).

Now begin work on the questions.

GO ON TO THE NEXT PAGE

2 2 2 2 2 2 2 2

1. Cyberspace is the world generated
   ------- computers and, however
   intangible, could well be the
   battlefield of the future.

   (A) of communicating
   (B) by communicating
   (C) to communicate
   (D) communicating

2. All major banks regularly have their
   computer systems illegally penetrated
   but rarely reveal it ------- bad
   publicity.

   (A) because
   (B) and for
   (C) due to
   (D) for fear of

3. Soft war is the ability ------- the
   perceptions of the enemy using media
   control to manipulate the images and
   messages received from the outside
   world.

   (A) changing
   (B) to change
   (C) which changing
   (D) with change

4. Pentagon computers zeroed in on
   Gaddafi's bank account and, within
   two minutes, ------- entire contents
   to a Washington bank.

   (A) transferring its
   (B) had transferred its
   (C) is transferring its
   (D) transferred it's

5. The mere threat of the Star Wars
   project did more to overcome the
   Soviets than ------- in the US
   arsenal.

   (A) to fear of any weapon
   (B) they feared any weapon
   (C) fear of any weapon
   (D) fearing of any weapon

6. Non-lethal weaponry, already being
   used by many US police forces,
   ------- into bloodless, computer-
   controlled struggles.

   (A) are turning war
   (B) which will turn war
   (C) and will turn war
   (D) will turn war

7. The monkey uses its tail -------
   balancing on a high branch and as an
   extra limb to help it swing from tree
   to tree.

   (A) trying
   (B) when
   (C) so
   (D) for to

8. The Anti-terrorist Act of 1973 linked
   foreign aid to the respect shown for
   human rights but ------- when it was
   in the best interests of the US to turn
   a blind eye.

   (A) excluded linkage
   (B) included linkage
   (C) exclusion of linkage
   (D) was excluding linkage

9. ------- thought and careful planning
   was behind the US invasion of Haiti.

   (A) There was much
   (B) Many
   (C) It was much
   (D) Much

GO ON TO THE NEXT PAGE

② ② ② ② ② ② ② ②

10. ------- Bill Gates, the young billionaire boss of Microsoft, used unscrupulous means to succeed is legendary but he still managed to retain the loyalty of his workers.

    (A) That
    (B) Because
    (C) While
    (D) Being

11. Now available in bookshops all over Russia, -------

    (A) Gurchenov wrote books that were once banned.
    (B) the books Gurchenov is writing were once banned.
    (C) Gurchenov's writing of books was once banned.
    (D) the books Gurchenov wrote were once banned.

12. The Bedouins of Israel, despite their Arab ancestry and common language, trust the Jews ------- the Palestinians.

    (A) more than they do
    (B) than they do more
    (C) more do they than
    (D) the more they do than

13. By writing such articles, ------- them in print blocks and publishing them in his own newspaper, Wilbert Owens lured many eastern city dwellers to the Wild West.

    (A) for to set
    (B) setting
    (C) and setting
    (D) while setting

14. Although well known by name throughout the world, Edison spent almost all his time in the laboratory and hardly ever ------- any of his admirers.

    (A) he did meet
    (B) did he meet
    (C) was he meeting
    (D) does he meet

15. The myth ------- an elephants' graveyard arose from their instinct to wander away from the herd when they sense their death approaching.

    (A) of there being
    (B) is there is
    (C) that their is
    (D) which is

GO ON TO THE NEXT PAGE

②②②②②②②②

Written Expression

Directions: In questions 16-40 each sentence has four underlined words or phrases. The four underlined parts of the sentence are marked (A), (B), (C), and (D). Identify the one underlined word or phrase that must be changed in order for the sentence to be correct. Then, on your answer sheet, find the number of the question and fill in the space that corresponds to the letter of the answer you have chosen.

Example I

Sample Answer

Ⓐ Ⓑ ● Ⓓ

Because of the storm all fifteen of the car failed
    A   B   C

to reach the check point.
   D

The sentence should read, "Because of the storm all fifteen of the cars failed to reach the check point." Therefore, you should choose (C).

Example II

Sample Answer

Ⓐ ● Ⓒ Ⓓ

The development of the attack helicopter begins at
         A   B

the end of last year and was completed within six
    C   D

months.

The sentence should read, "The development of the attack helicopter began at the end of last year and was completed within six months." Therefore, you should choose (B).

Now begin work on the questions.

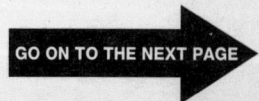

GO ON TO THE NEXT PAGE

56

② ② ② ② ② ② ② ②

16. Never in the history of the US military it has been so powerful yet had such an
            A   B   C
    uncertain function in the world.
          D

17. Bright, vivid colors and evocative, thought-provoke designs are the hallmark of
        A   B   C
    Liechtenstein's works of art.
          D

18. With both baseball players and club managers earning a hundred times the national
        A   B
    average wage, the strike of 1994 was more due from greed than need.
          C   D

19. Kinnock's revelations lends credence to the theory that AIDS was deliberately let
                         A   B
    loose in the community to eradicate homosexuals and intravenous drug users.
      C   D

20. The canal system was opened in the turn of the century and, as a direct result,
          A   B   C
    Chicago grew to be one of the most prosperous cities of the north.
          D

21. Cod, once one of the most plentiful species of fish, is now almost a rarity as their
          A   B   C
    breeding grounds have been decimated by over-fishing.
          D

22. Because of the bombing of free clinics in Arkansas and the shooting of doctors,
                                      A
    analysis subjective of the abortion issue has been constantly hindered.
      B   C   D

23. Faced with the possibility of defeat in Sicily, General Patton defied Eisenhower's
      A   B
    orders, commanding the army to assemble it's forces on the south coast.
          C   D

24. Rasputin, a wandering Russian monk, gained immense power over Tsar Nicholas in
          A   B   C
    the years before 1917 revolution.
          D

GO ON TO THE NEXT PAGE

2 2 2 2 2 2 2 2

25. Roosevelt's National Recovery Administration, established in 1933 by a special
<u>A</u>
mandate, empowered the federal government to shorten working hours,
<u>B</u>
improve wages and also to end the employment of children.
<u>C</u>   <u>D</u>

26. Vaccination <u>was developed</u> <u>from</u> Edward Jenner in about 1796 <u>and involved</u> the
<u>A</u>   <u>B</u>   <u>C</u>
injection of dead or <u>weak</u> bacteria into the bloodstream.
<u>D</u>

27. Che Guevara, <u>an Argentinean</u> doctor, <u>who became</u> one of the leaders of the Cuban
<u>A</u>   <u>B</u>
revolution and <u>encouraged</u> revolution <u>throughout</u> Latin America.
<u>C</u>   <u>D</u>

28. A US policy meeting <u>on</u> June 1, 1945 <u>recommended</u> that the atomic bomb
<u>A</u>   <u>B</u>
<u>be dropped</u> on a Japanese military base but President Truman <u>was electing</u> to use it
<u>C</u>   <u>D</u>
against the civil target of Hiroshima.

29. Hong Kong <u>was seized</u> by the British in 1841 <u>during</u> a war <u>waged</u> for the right
<u>A</u>   <u>B</u>   <u>C</u>
<u>to sell</u> opium to the Chinese is not disputed.
<u>D</u>

30. Insulin is a substance <u>which is produced</u> in the <u>pancreatic gland</u> of human beings
<u>A</u>   <u>B</u>   <u>C</u>
and <u>much</u> of the world's mammals.
<u>D</u>

31. <u>Roosevelt</u> became the <u>26th</u> President of the United States <u>as</u> William McKinley
<u>A</u>   <u>B</u>   <u>C</u>
<u>was assassinated</u> in 1901.
<u>D</u>

32. The <u>Salvation Army</u>, a non-governmental body <u>seeking to preach</u> the Christian
<u>A</u>   <u>B</u>
gospel, was <u>given it's name</u> by William Booth in 1878.
<u>C</u>   <u>D</u>

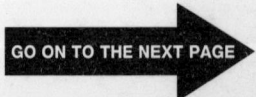

GO ON TO THE NEXT PAGE

② ② ② ② ② ② ② ②

33. By 1913, Albert Schweitzer, a newly qualified doctor, sailed for Africa to work with
    A   B

    the underprivileged but it wasn't until 1953 that his work was recognized and he
               C   D

    was awarded a Nobel Prize.

34. The Suez Canal, completed in 1869 after ten years of work directed by Ferdinand de
    A   B   C

    Lesseps, was widened and there was deepening in 1886.
                                D

35. The first usable telephone depended on electro-magnetism was invented by
        A   B   C

    Alexander Bell in 1876.
            D

36. A 1975 US Senate investigation reported that the CIA had encouraged plots
                            A   B

    to destabilize countries and had actively participation in many conspiracies to
         C   D

    murder foreign leaders.

37. Conscription, the drafting of recruits for compulsory military service, is
        A   B

    unlikely to be reinstated because of the nature specialized of modern
                  C   D

    soldiering.

38. Marie Curie, the discoverer of radium, came to Paris in 1891 because of
                    A   B

    her revolutionary views made it impossible for her to stay in her
                            C

    native Poland.
        D

GO ON TO THE NEXT PAGE

② ② ② ② ② ② ② ②

39. In spite his reactionary views and intolerance toward moral lapses, it is now clear
    <u>   </u>   <u>   </u>
        A   B
    that J Edgar Hoover was secretly a practicing homosexual throughout his career
                       <u>   </u>
                              C
    as the head of the FBI.
    <u>   </u>
              D

40. Having defeated his Turkish enemies, Ataturk then defeated the Greeks and
    <u>   </u>   <u>   </u>
          A   B
    literally thrusted them back into the sea.
    <u>   </u> <u>   </u>
          C   D

This is the end of Section 2.

If you finish in less than 25 minutes, check your work on Section 2 only.
Do NOT read or work on any other section of the test.

STOP STOP STOP **STOP** STOP STOP STOP

At the end of 25 minutes, go on to Section 3.

Use *exactly 55 minutes* to work on Section 3.

TEST OF ENGLISH AS A FOREIGN LANGUAGE

Practice Answer Sheet
Horizontal Format

Section 1	Section 2	Section 3
1 Ⓐ Ⓑ Ⓒ Ⓓ	1 Ⓐ Ⓑ Ⓒ Ⓓ	1 Ⓐ Ⓑ Ⓒ Ⓓ
2 Ⓐ Ⓑ Ⓒ Ⓓ	2 Ⓐ Ⓑ Ⓒ Ⓓ	2 Ⓐ Ⓑ Ⓒ Ⓓ
3 Ⓐ Ⓑ Ⓒ Ⓓ	3 Ⓐ Ⓑ Ⓒ Ⓓ	3 Ⓐ Ⓑ Ⓒ Ⓓ
4 Ⓐ Ⓑ Ⓒ Ⓓ	4 Ⓐ Ⓑ Ⓒ Ⓓ	4 Ⓐ Ⓑ Ⓒ Ⓓ
5 Ⓐ Ⓑ Ⓒ Ⓓ	5 Ⓐ Ⓑ Ⓒ Ⓓ	5 Ⓐ Ⓑ Ⓒ Ⓓ
6 Ⓐ Ⓑ Ⓒ Ⓓ	6 Ⓐ Ⓑ Ⓒ Ⓓ	6 Ⓐ Ⓑ Ⓒ Ⓓ
7 Ⓐ Ⓑ Ⓒ Ⓓ	7 Ⓐ Ⓑ Ⓒ Ⓓ	7 Ⓐ Ⓑ Ⓒ Ⓓ
8 Ⓐ Ⓑ Ⓒ Ⓓ	8 Ⓐ Ⓑ Ⓒ Ⓓ	8 Ⓐ Ⓑ Ⓒ Ⓓ
9 Ⓐ Ⓑ Ⓒ Ⓓ	9 Ⓐ Ⓑ Ⓒ Ⓓ	9 Ⓐ Ⓑ Ⓒ Ⓓ
10 Ⓐ Ⓑ Ⓒ Ⓓ	10 Ⓐ Ⓑ Ⓒ Ⓓ	10 Ⓐ Ⓑ Ⓒ Ⓓ
11 Ⓐ Ⓑ Ⓒ Ⓓ	11 Ⓐ Ⓑ Ⓒ Ⓓ	11 Ⓐ Ⓑ Ⓒ Ⓓ
12 Ⓐ Ⓑ Ⓒ Ⓓ	12 Ⓐ Ⓑ Ⓒ Ⓓ	12 Ⓐ Ⓑ Ⓒ Ⓓ
13 Ⓐ Ⓑ Ⓒ Ⓓ	13 Ⓐ Ⓑ Ⓒ Ⓓ	13 Ⓐ Ⓑ Ⓒ Ⓓ
14 Ⓐ Ⓑ Ⓒ Ⓓ	14 Ⓐ Ⓑ Ⓒ Ⓓ	14 Ⓐ Ⓑ Ⓒ Ⓓ
15 Ⓐ Ⓑ Ⓒ Ⓓ	15 Ⓐ Ⓑ Ⓒ Ⓓ	15 Ⓐ Ⓑ Ⓒ Ⓓ
16 Ⓐ Ⓑ Ⓒ Ⓓ	16 Ⓐ Ⓑ Ⓒ Ⓓ	16 Ⓐ Ⓑ Ⓒ Ⓓ
17 Ⓐ Ⓑ Ⓒ Ⓓ	17 Ⓐ Ⓑ Ⓒ Ⓓ	17 Ⓐ Ⓑ Ⓒ Ⓓ
18 Ⓐ Ⓑ Ⓒ Ⓓ	18 Ⓐ Ⓑ Ⓒ Ⓓ	18 Ⓐ Ⓑ Ⓒ Ⓓ
19 Ⓐ Ⓑ Ⓒ Ⓓ	19 Ⓐ Ⓑ Ⓒ Ⓓ	19 Ⓐ Ⓑ Ⓒ Ⓓ
20 Ⓐ Ⓑ Ⓒ Ⓓ	20 Ⓐ Ⓑ Ⓒ Ⓓ	20 Ⓐ Ⓑ Ⓒ Ⓓ
21 Ⓐ Ⓑ Ⓒ Ⓓ	21 Ⓐ Ⓑ Ⓒ Ⓓ	21 Ⓐ Ⓑ Ⓒ Ⓓ
22 Ⓐ Ⓑ Ⓒ Ⓓ	22 Ⓐ Ⓑ Ⓒ Ⓓ	22 Ⓐ Ⓑ Ⓒ Ⓓ
23 Ⓐ Ⓑ Ⓒ Ⓓ	23 Ⓐ Ⓑ Ⓒ Ⓓ	23 Ⓐ Ⓑ Ⓒ Ⓓ
24 Ⓐ Ⓑ Ⓒ Ⓓ	24 Ⓐ Ⓑ Ⓒ Ⓓ	24 Ⓐ Ⓑ Ⓒ Ⓓ
25 Ⓐ Ⓑ Ⓒ Ⓓ	25 Ⓐ Ⓑ Ⓒ Ⓓ	25 Ⓐ Ⓑ Ⓒ Ⓓ
26 Ⓐ Ⓑ Ⓒ Ⓓ	26 Ⓐ Ⓑ Ⓒ Ⓓ	26 Ⓐ Ⓑ Ⓒ Ⓓ
27 Ⓐ Ⓑ Ⓒ Ⓓ	27 Ⓐ Ⓑ Ⓒ Ⓓ	27 Ⓐ Ⓑ Ⓒ Ⓓ
28 Ⓐ Ⓑ Ⓒ Ⓓ	28 Ⓐ Ⓑ Ⓒ Ⓓ	28 Ⓐ Ⓑ Ⓒ Ⓓ
29 Ⓐ Ⓑ Ⓒ Ⓓ	29 Ⓐ Ⓑ Ⓒ Ⓓ	29 Ⓐ Ⓑ Ⓒ Ⓓ
30 Ⓐ Ⓑ Ⓒ Ⓓ	30 Ⓐ Ⓑ Ⓒ Ⓓ	30 Ⓐ Ⓑ Ⓒ Ⓓ
31 Ⓐ Ⓑ Ⓒ Ⓓ	31 Ⓐ Ⓑ Ⓒ Ⓓ	31 Ⓐ Ⓑ Ⓒ Ⓓ
32 Ⓐ Ⓑ Ⓒ Ⓓ	32 Ⓐ Ⓑ Ⓒ Ⓓ	32 Ⓐ Ⓑ Ⓒ Ⓓ
33 Ⓐ Ⓑ Ⓒ Ⓓ	33 Ⓐ Ⓑ Ⓒ Ⓓ	33 Ⓐ Ⓑ Ⓒ Ⓓ
34 Ⓐ Ⓑ Ⓒ Ⓓ	34 Ⓐ Ⓑ Ⓒ Ⓓ	34 Ⓐ Ⓑ Ⓒ Ⓓ
35 Ⓐ Ⓑ Ⓒ Ⓓ	35 Ⓐ Ⓑ Ⓒ Ⓓ	35 Ⓐ Ⓑ Ⓒ Ⓓ
36 Ⓐ Ⓑ Ⓒ Ⓓ	36 Ⓐ Ⓑ Ⓒ Ⓓ	36 Ⓐ Ⓑ Ⓒ Ⓓ
37 Ⓐ Ⓑ Ⓒ Ⓓ	37 Ⓐ Ⓑ Ⓒ Ⓓ	37 Ⓐ Ⓑ Ⓒ Ⓓ
38 Ⓐ Ⓑ Ⓒ Ⓓ	38 Ⓐ Ⓑ Ⓒ Ⓓ	38 Ⓐ Ⓑ Ⓒ Ⓓ
39 Ⓐ Ⓑ Ⓒ Ⓓ	39 Ⓐ Ⓑ Ⓒ Ⓓ	39 Ⓐ Ⓑ Ⓒ Ⓓ
40 Ⓐ Ⓑ Ⓒ Ⓓ	40 Ⓐ Ⓑ Ⓒ Ⓓ	40 Ⓐ Ⓑ Ⓒ Ⓓ
41 Ⓐ Ⓑ Ⓒ Ⓓ		41 Ⓐ Ⓑ Ⓒ Ⓓ
42 Ⓐ Ⓑ Ⓒ Ⓓ		42 Ⓐ Ⓑ Ⓒ Ⓓ
43 Ⓐ Ⓑ Ⓒ Ⓓ		43 Ⓐ Ⓑ Ⓒ Ⓓ
44 Ⓐ Ⓑ Ⓒ Ⓓ		44 Ⓐ Ⓑ Ⓒ Ⓓ
45 Ⓐ Ⓑ Ⓒ Ⓓ		45 Ⓐ Ⓑ Ⓒ Ⓓ
46 Ⓐ Ⓑ Ⓒ Ⓓ		46 Ⓐ Ⓑ Ⓒ Ⓓ
47 Ⓐ Ⓑ Ⓒ Ⓓ		47 Ⓐ Ⓑ Ⓒ Ⓓ
48 Ⓐ Ⓑ Ⓒ Ⓓ		48 Ⓐ Ⓑ Ⓒ Ⓓ
49 Ⓐ Ⓑ Ⓒ Ⓓ		49 Ⓐ Ⓑ Ⓒ Ⓓ
50 Ⓐ Ⓑ Ⓒ Ⓓ		50 Ⓐ Ⓑ Ⓒ Ⓓ

TEST OF ENGLISH AS A FOREIGN LANGUAGE

Practice Answer Sheet

Vertical Format

Section 1

1 (A) (B) (C) (D)
2 (A) (B) (C) (D)
3 (A) (B) (C) (D)
4 (A) (B) (C) (D)
5 (A) (B) (C) (D)
6 (A) (B) (C) (D)
7 (A) (B) (C) (D)
8 (A) (B) (C) (D)
9 (A) (B) (C) (D)
10 (A) (B) (C) (D)
11 (A) (B) (C) (D)
12 (A) (B) (C) (D)
13 (A) (B) (C) (D)
14 (A) (B) (C) (D)
15 (A) (B) (C) (D)
16 (A) (B) (C) (D)
17 (A) (B) (C) (D)
18 (A) (B) (C) (D)
19 (A) (B) (C) (D)
20 (A) (B) (C) (D)
21 (A) (B) (C) (D)
22 (A) (B) (C) (D)
23 (A) (B) (C) (D)
24 (A) (B) (C) (D)
25 (A) (B) (C) (D)
26 (A) (B) (C) (D)
27 (A) (B) (C) (D)
28 (A) (B) (C) (D)
29 (A) (B) (C) (D)
30 (A) (B) (C) (D)
31 (A) (B) (C) (D)
32 (A) (B) (C) (D)
33 (A) (B) (C) (D)
34 (A) (B) (C) (D)
35 (A) (B) (C) (D)
36 (A) (B) (C) (D)
37 (A) (B) (C) (D)
38 (A) (B) (C) (D)
39 (A) (B) (C) (D)
40 (A) (B) (C) (D)
41 (A) (B) (C) (D)
42 (A) (B) (C) (D)
43 (A) (B) (C) (D)
44 (A) (B) (C) (D)
45 (A) (B) (C) (D)
46 (A) (B) (C) (D)
47 (A) (B) (C) (D)
48 (A) (B) (C) (D)
49 (A) (B) (C) (D)
50 (A) (B) (C) (D)

Section 2

1 (A) (B) (C) (D)
2 (A) (B) (C) (D)
3 (A) (B) (C) (D)
4 (A) (B) (C) (D)
5 (A) (B) (C) (D)
6 (A) (B) (C) (D)
7 (A) (B) (C) (D)
8 (A) (B) (C) (D)
9 (A) (B) (C) (D)
10 (A) (B) (C) (D)
11 (A) (B) (C) (D)
12 (A) (B) (C) (D)
13 (A) (B) (C) (D)
14 (A) (B) (C) (D)
15 (A) (B) (C) (D)
16 (A) (B) (C) (D)
17 (A) (B) (C) (D)
18 (A) (B) (C) (D)
19 (A) (B) (C) (D)
20 (A) (B) (C) (D)
21 (A) (B) (C) (D)
22 (A) (B) (C) (D)
23 (A) (B) (C) (D)
24 (A) (B) (C) (D)
25 (A) (B) (C) (D)
26 (A) (B) (C) (D)
27 (A) (B) (C) (D)
28 (A) (B) (C) (D)
29 (A) (B) (C) (D)
30 (A) (B) (C) (D)
31 (A) (B) (C) (D)
32 (A) (B) (C) (D)
33 (A) (B) (C) (D)
34 (A) (B) (C) (D)
35 (A) (B) (C) (D)
36 (A) (B) (C) (D)
37 (A) (B) (C) (D)
38 (A) (B) (C) (D)
39 (A) (B) (C) (D)
40 (A) (B) (C) (D)

Section 3

1 (A) (B) (C) (D)
2 (A) (B) (C) (D)
3 (A) (B) (C) (D)
4 (A) (B) (C) (D)
5 (A) (B) (C) (D)
6 (A) (B) (C) (D)
7 (A) (B) (C) (D)
8 (A) (B) (C) (D)
9 (A) (B) (C) (D)
10 (A) (B) (C) (D)
11 (A) (B) (C) (D)
12 (A) (B) (C) (D)
13 (A) (B) (C) (D)
14 (A) (B) (C) (D)
15 (A) (B) (C) (D)
16 (A) (B) (C) (D)
17 (A) (B) (C) (D)
18 (A) (B) (C) (D)
19 (A) (B) (C) (D)
20 (A) (B) (C) (D)
21 (A) (B) (C) (D)
22 (A) (B) (C) (D)
23 (A) (B) (C) (D)
24 (A) (B) (C) (D)
25 (A) (B) (C) (D)
26 (A) (B) (C) (D)
27 (A) (B) (C) (D)
28 (A) (B) (C) (D)
29 (A) (B) (C) (D)
30 (A) (B) (C) (D)
31 (A) (B) (C) (D)
32 (A) (B) (C) (D)
33 (A) (B) (C) (D)
34 (A) (B) (C) (D)
35 (A) (B) (C) (D)
36 (A) (B) (C) (D)
37 (A) (B) (C) (D)
38 (A) (B) (C) (D)
39 (A) (B) (C) (D)
40 (A) (B) (C) (D)
41 (A) (B) (C) (D)
42 (A) (B) (C) (D)
43 (A) (B) (C) (D)
44 (A) (B) (C) (D)
45 (A) (B) (C) (D)
46 (A) (B) (C) (D)
47 (A) (B) (C) (D)
48 (A) (B) (C) (D)
49 (A) (B) (C) (D)
50 (A) (B) (C) (D)

TOEFL ANSWER KEY

Test One	Test Two	Test Three	Test Four	Test Five	Test Six	Test Seven
1. A	1. B	1. D	1. D	1. C	1. C	1. B
2. C	2. D	2. A	2. D	2. C	2. B	2. D
3. A	3. B	3. B	3. A	3. C	3. B	3. B
4. A	4. A	4. D	4. B	4. C	4. B	4. B
5. D	5. B	5. C	5. B	5. C	5. D	5. C
6. A	6. D	6. D	6. A	6. D	6. B	6. D
7. D	7. A	7. B	7. D	7. C	7. D	7. B
8. A	8. D	8. C	8. B	8. B	8. D	8. A
9. B	9. C	9. D	9. B	9. A	9. D	9. D
10. C	10. B	10. B	10. D	10. D	10. B	10. A
11. A	11. C	11. D	11. D	11. D	11. A	11. D
12. B	12. C	12. D	12. D	12. D	12. D	12. A
13. A	13. D	13. A	13. C	13. B	13. D	13. B
14. D	14. B	14. D	14. C	14. B	14. A	14. B
15. D	15. C	15. B	15. A	15. C	15. D	15. A
16. D	16. C	16. D	16. B	16. B	16. C	16. B
17. D	17. B	17. A	17. C	17. C	17. A	17. B
18. C	18. D	18. A	18. D	18. A	18. B	18. D
19. B	19. C	19. C	19. B	19. D	19. B	19. A
20. B	20. D	20. B	20. B	20. C	20. B	20. B
21. D	21. D	21. D	21. A	21. D	21. D	21. C
22. C	22. C	22. B	22. B	22. A	22. D	22. B
23. B	23. D	23. D	23. D	23. C	23. C	23. D
24. D	24. D	24. D	24. D	24. D	24. C	24. D
25. C	25. A	25. C	25. A	25. D	25. A	25. D
26. D	26. D	26. C	26. C	26. D	26. A	26. B
27. B	27. C	27. C	27. B	27. A	27. C	27. B
28. A	28. D	28. C	28. C	28. B	28. D	28. D
29. A	29. D	29. C	29. D	29. C	29. D	29. A
30. C	30. A	30. D	30. B	30. B	30. C	30. D
31. A	31. C	31. D	31. A	31. B	31. A	31. C
32. A	32. A	32. D	32. C	32. D	32. B	32. C
33. D	33. C	33. D	33. C	33. B	33. D	33. A
34. A	34. C	34. A	34. B	34. C	34. C	34. C
35. C	35. A	35. A	35. C	35. B	35. B	35. B
36. A	36. A	36. B	36. D	36. A	36. B	36. D
37. D	37. D	37. A	37. A	37. D	37. C	37. D
38. A	38. D	38. D	38. D	38. D	38. C	38. B
39. B	39. C	39. B	39. B	39. B	39. C	39. A
40. A	40. C	40. C	40. B	40. C	40. D	40. C

Scoring Your Practice Tests

When your TOEFL tests are scored, you will receive a score of between 20 and 70 for each of the three sections (Listening Comprehension, Structure and Written Expression, Reading Comprehension). You will also receive an overall score of between 200 and 700.

You can use the following charts to estimate your scores on your practice TOEFL tests.

Use the following chart to estimate your score on the practice Listening Comprehension tests and the practice Reading Comprehension tests:

Number of Correct Answers	Converted Score	Number of Correct Answers	Converted Score	Number of Correct Answers	Converted Score	Number of Correct Answers	Converted Score
50	68	37	54	24	46	11	36
49	66	36	53	23	45	10	35
48	64	35	53	22	45	9	33
47	63	34	52	21	44	8	32
46	62	33	51	20	43	7	31
45	61	32	51	19	43	6	30
44	60	31	50	18	42	5	29
43	59	30	49	17	42	4	28
42	58	29	49	16	41	3	27
41	57	28	48	15	40	2	25
40	57	27	48	14	39	1	22
39	56	26	47	13	38	0	20
38	55	25	46	12	37		

Use the following chart to estimate your score on the practice Structure and Written Expression tests:

Number of Correct Answers	Converted Score	Number of Correct Answers	Converted Score	Number of Correct Answers	Converted Score	Number of Correct Answers	Converted Score
40	68	29	52	18	41	7	30
39	65	28	51	17	40	6	28
38	64	27	50	16	39	5	26
37	63	26	49	15	38	4	25
36	61	25	48	14	37	3	24
35	59	24	47	13	36	2	23
34	58	23	46	12	35	1	21
33	57	22	45	11	34	0	20
32	56	21	44	10	34		
31	54	20	43	9	33		
30	53	19	42	8	31		

Once you have worked out your converted score for each of the three test sections, you can then determine your overall score by adding the three converted scores together, dividing the sum by three and then multiplying by ten. So for example, imagine your scores were as follows:

	Number of Correct Answers	Converted Score
Section 1	32	51
Section 2	33	57
Section 3	37	54

Add the converted scores together: 51 + 57 + 54 = 162
Divide the sum by three: 162 ÷ 3 = 54
Multiply by ten: 54 x 10 = 540

So the overall TOEFL score in this example is 540.